Simply: The Nester's brilliant. I couldn't stop reading. Seth Godin meets Martha Stewart meets Emilie Barnes — this is one wise, real, winsome book you can't put down and will be picking up years from now. These pages will have you making more than the home you dreamed of. They will have you receiving the *life* you always dreamed of.

— ANN VOSKAMP, *New York Times* bestselling author of
One Thousand Gifts: A Dare to Live Fully Right Where You Are

My family and I move around quite a bit, so we're quite used to transforming houses of all types into homes. But I think I've still held on to the fear of messing up, hammering in "too many" nail holes, and generally having a home that's just a bit too imperfect. Well, *The Nesting Place* is the perfect cheerleader I need to take risks in my house, so that it can be the place it needs to be — home for those of us who live there. Myquillyn's big-sister approach is encouraging, hilarious, and heartwarming, just the kind of house book I love. So many families will be encouraged by her words. I'm so glad she's shared them with us.

— TSH OXENREIDER, author of *Notes from a Blue Bike:
The Art of Living Intentionally in a Chaotic World*

This highly personal account about embracing imperfection and finding content-ment in your home is like sitting down with a good friend and talking about the stuff that really matters. *The Nesting Place* is full of approachable ideas, encouragement, and a whole lot of heart.

— SHERRY PETERSIK, home blogger and bestselling
author of *Young House Love*

If you're anything like me, the words, "It doesn't have to be perfect to be beautiful," sum up more than my approach to design. In this gorgeous book, you'll see that Myquillyn lives it out in a spectacularly inspiring and yet inviting way — a rare combination of gifts. I laughed at her recollections of previous homes and stared wistfully at my own walls, willing them to grow antlers or a collection of frames before I finished reading. She has the ability to sit beside you with her words as a gentle, kind, inspired friend, and to urge you to make a space your own — not just for the sake of paint or furniture, but because it's good medicine for the heart to feel at home. She's a storyteller, a do-it-yourselfer, a God-chaser, and a woman who knows what it's like to put down roots wherever the Lord has planted her and grow them into something beautiful. I know you'll love her the same way I do, so open the pages and let her words plant a seed wherever you are.

— ANGIE SMITH, Women of Faith speaker and bestselling
author of *I Will Carry You*; *What Women Fear*; *Mended*; and
Chasing God

Confession: making my home beautiful and inviting has always been intimidating. *The Nesting Place* makes me feel like I have not only my own personal decorator but also an encouraging friend beside me. Whew.

> — HOLLEY GERTH, bestselling author of *You're Already Amazing*

Growing up I always wished my sister would play Barbies the "right" way — make them have conversations and relationships and drama. Instead, all she wanted to do was set up their pink plastic houses. Now we're all grown up, and as I read her words in *The Nesting Place*, it all finally makes sense.

Myquillyn is the home evangelist to the tired perfectionist, and what she preaches is permission — to make ourselves at home right where we are.

If you have ever felt like you're waiting for your next place to be the home you've always dreamed of, I beg you to read this encouraging, personal, hilarious book and let the Nester change your mind. It doesn't have to be fancy, expensive, complicated, designer, or perfect to be beautiful.

> — EMILY P. FREEMAN, the Nester's little sister and author of *A Million Little Ways*

The Nesting Place is so much more than a decorating book. Each chapter is packed with creative insights that helped me define my personal style and discover hidden beauty in my home. But also, without meaning to, Myquillyn helped me see hidden beauty in my life in the most unexpected ways. Her personal experiences had me laughing, and her practical ideas had me daydreaming about rooms in my house that could be made new through simple yet brilliant ideas that fill the whole book. If you've longed for a friend to walk through your home and help you see beyond obstacles to the full potential of the spaces you live in, *The Nesting Place* is for you.

> — RENEE SWOPE, Proverbs 31 Ministries radio show cohost and bestselling author of *A Confident Heart*

This book made me look at every room in my house differently, with a new lens of creativity and beauty and possibility. It inspired me to reclaim my home as sacred space, ripe with opportunities to celebrate and create memories and moments.

> — SHAUNA NIEQUIST, author of *Bread & Wine*

The

NESTING
PLACE

The

NESTING PLACE

It Doesn't Have to Be Perfect to *Be Beautiful*

"THE NESTER"

ZONDERVAN
BOOKS

ZONDERVAN BOOKS

The Nesting Place
Copyright © 2014 by Myquillyn Smith

Requests for information should be addressed to:
Zondervan, 3900 *Sparks Dr. SE, Grand Rapids, Michigan 49546*

Zondervan titles may be purchased in bulk for educational, business, fundraising, or sales promotional use. For information, please email SpecialMarkets@Zondervan.com.

ISBN 978-0-310-36095-7 (hardcover)

ISBN 978-0-310-36215-9 (audio)

The Library of Congress has cataloged the original edition as follows:

Smith, Myquillyn.
    The nesting place : your home doesn't have to be perfect to be beautiful / Myquillyn Smith.
      pages cm
    ISBN 978-0-310-33790-4 (hardcover) — ISBN 978-0-310-33791-1 (ebook)
    1. Home — Religious aspects — Christianity. 2. Home economics. 3. Rental housing. I. Title.
    BR115.H56S65 2014
    248.4'6 — dc23   2013034145

Scripture quotations are taken from the Good News Translation® (Today's English Version, Second Edition), Copyright © 1992 by American Bible Society. All rights reserved.

Any internet addresses (websites, blogs, etc.) and telephone numbers in this book are offered as a resource. They are not intended in any way to be or imply an endorsement by Zondervan, nor does Zondervan vouch for the content of these sites and numbers for the life of this book.

Published in association with the literary agency of The Fedd Agency, Post Office Box 341973, Austin, TX 78734.

Cover design: Curt Diepenhorst
Photography: Myquillyn Smith
Interior design: Jody Langley

Printed in Malaysia

20 21 22 23 24 25 26 27 28 /IMAGO/ 23 22 21 20 19 18 17 16 15 14 13 12 11 10 9 8 7 6 5 4 3 2 1

FOR YOU,
because every house has a silver lining

BECAUSE OF CHAD,
the most encouraging man in the world

INSPIRED BY HEATHER,
who taught me that life doesn't have to be
perfect to be wonderful

IN HONOR OF LANDIS, CADEMON, AND GAVIN:
home is wherever you are

IN MEMORY OF GRANDMA MORLAND
AND MELISSA COLE:
growing up, your homes were
my favorite places to be

Contents

Where thou art,
that is home.

— EMILY DICKINSON

CHAPTER 1

The Before

A LOVED-ON AND LIVED-IN
twelve-dollar thrifted chair with
a broken leg and a homemade
slipcover. Coziness at its finest.

A beautiful thing is never perfect.

— ANCIENT PROVERB

Dwelling in Possibility

As a child, I didn't have huge dreams, impressive ambitions, or fancy prayers. I was a simple girl who looked forward to having a family and settling down in a little white house and growing something — you know, like a garden.

Compared with what other people were asking of God, I figured my request for a quiet life would be pretty easy to fill. But you know what happened?

The opposite.

My husband and I have moved 734 times in our marriage. Actually, it's been thirteen times in eighteen years of being married, but as my fellow frequent movers know, each move can feel like ten moves. Only one house was white, and that's because I paid to have it painted white. Six months later, we had to move out.

Along the way, we've lost two businesses, had a disgusting amount of debt, and been embarrassed by what all this did to our credit. Every time I decided to plant peonies or hydrangeas, we moved before they bloomed. We have not settled down into a cozy little white house. We have not really settled down at all.

I didn't think it was fair that we had to move so much, but I couldn't complain. Our kids were healthy, my husband was supportive, and it didn't seem very Jesus-y to fret over a house.

Maybe you've been there too.

I finally realized that maybe all the junk I didn't like about our lives was part of a story, a story with an ending I'd like even if it wasn't what I had imagined.

Those thirteen homes weren't a waste. They were teaching me valuable lessons and I almost missed it. I almost gave up and believed the lie that loving the home you are in is reserved for a few lucky people whose circumstances happen to work out just right.

As a renter, I've always felt like the unreached people group of the design world.

FOR YEARS I wanted a cuckoo clock. One day this turned up on my porch, a gift from a friend. She found it at a yard sale for ten dollars.

CANVAS with all of our
past street names

"Someday" Is Now

Have you given up on the idea that you can love your home? Do you find yourself thinking that your next house will be the one you love? Do you put off decorating projects until "someday" because someday you'll have time and money to do it "right"? And yet do you long to create a beautiful home for more than beauty's sake?

I sense a restlessness among women — my neighbors, my online friends, and most of all, myself. We desire something more than the next DIY craze or perfectly decorated space. We want to truly love, appreciate, and use our homes. We don't want to put a bandaid on something we hate, no matter how cute and budget-friendly that bandaid may be. But we don't know where to start. And hey, we are smart women; we also crave a sense of balance. Yes, we enjoy beauty and love a pretty room, but we aren't willing to destroy our finances or realign our priorities to get there.

Creating a beautiful home is a journey,
not a destination.

OPPOSITE While I was writing this book in my bed (don't judge), I got up and noticed the beauty in the midst of the everyday. Pink straws, blue polish, and earbuds can be beautiful too.

That's why this book isn't about decorating a house. It's about creating a beautiful, meaningful home that you love. Right where you are. It includes practical tips, but more important, it presents a philosophy of decorating that I've found so freeing that it guides every decorating decision I make in my own home.

Do you believe it's possible to love where you are, right now, today?

I promise, I have made every home-decorating mistake, and then some. I have spilled the gallon of discount paint on the floor of the rental. I have spilled the quart of expensive paint on the pretty shelf. I have broken the oversized mirror. I have regretted the fabric, I have measured once and cut twice, I have painted one room five different colors in two years, I have made too many nail holes, ripped the sofa, purchased the wrong size, and bought chandeliers that were too small. I have returned rugs and lamps and pillows. I've been there, ruined that. I have lived to tell. And my house is better for it.

In our thirteen houses, I have made every mistake. It's been the best education I could have asked for. If I'd never tried, my house would still look like it did eighteen years ago. I'd still be giving dirty looks to a plaid hand-me-down sofa.

For Renters, Transients, and Modern-Day Nomads

....

Reluctant Renters

As a renter, I've always felt like the unreached people group of the design world. We really aren't that much of a minority: one-third of Americans today rent their homes. Sure, there are all sorts of inspiring ideas for those singles in New York City leasing tiny lofts with exposed brick walls. But what about the suburban mom? What about someone like me who struggles with feeling second class as the renter in the subdivision with the HOA full of homeowners? What about the military family or the missionaries or the pastor's family living in the parsonage sometimes referred to as "the dilapidated shack next to the church"?

At times I've felt like renting was my dirty little secret and that I was just waiting on our next house so I could make it pretty. But not anymore. We've rented ten different homes in our past eighteen years of marriage, and I am finally content to rent.

Fellow renters, look for a few sections like this throughout the book with tips and advice just for you. And remember that the photos in this book all come from the home that we love and rent as I type these words.

....

Greater Purposes

In September of 2010, I got a gift in the mail from my friend Dee: a canvas with the names of all of the streets where we've lived (by Red Letter Words).

I opened it and bawled. I cried the ugly cry — the trembling, snotty, bloodshot-eyes cry. My husband, afraid and confused, told me I didn't have to display the canvas if it made me sad. Sad? What? Did this look sad to him? Clearly I was happy! Seeing all the street names in one place helped me see something that had been happening all along. Woven through each of our sad/happy/weird transitions was a story, and I was beginning to see what the story was about. Because with all that moving and debt and non-white-house living and discontentment and guilt about feeling discontent and living in rentals when I wanted to own, I still got what I was looking for: a home.

I can sit here today in our rental house and embrace where we live and declare that I'm content. Because I trust that even though this might not be the exact home I'd choose, God chose it for me, and it is home.

I don't have a little white house. I have a big subdivision-style plastic house. But the people I love are here. I don't have a garden. But things are growing. I don't have all the money or time I want to decorate. But I have enough to take risks, be a little quirky, and enjoy the process.

I love sharing my lived-in home with friends, online, and now with you through this book. I don't open my home because it's finally done and presentable. I share it for the same reason I wear a bikini to the pool. It's not because I think I look great in it. It's because I'm finally okay that I don't. It's the same with our home. I don't share it because it's perfect; I share it because I'm finally okay that it's not.

I can accept the fact that my house and life and body aren't perfect, because I trust there is a greater purpose. I trust that God knows what he's doing, and I don't have to panic and attempt to make sense of it all. I've given up trying to control our circumstances and instead am determined to create a home wherever we are. And that's made all the difference.

CHAPTER 2

Thirteen Homes and Counting

Carrington Pointe
Gosling Terrace
Spring House Place
Tower · Confederate Avenue
Clisby Baytree
Barrington Hall
Florence Court
Berkley Tomoka Oaks
Glenwyck Lane
Jefferson Terrace

dwell.

A GALLERY WALL full of inexpensive, handmade, and secondhand art hangs over a slipcovered six-year-old sofa and two thrifted tables.

An expert is a person who has made all the mistakes that can be made in a very narrow field.

— NIELS BOHR

From Dumps to Mansions and Everything In-Between

I'm an expert in creating a beautiful home, but not because I'm highly trained with my one year of community-college design classes. I'm an expert because I've had practice in thirteen homes so far and I've learned from each one, especially the ones I've hated and wasted time whining about. I am an expert because I finally love our home and think it's beautiful. But getting there wasn't easy.

Houses 1 and 2: The Bachelor Townhouse and the House with the Pink Carpet

It was 1995, my husband, Chad, and I were freshly married, and my lifelong dream was coming true: we were buying our first house. This was going to be the second house we had ever lived in together. Chad was renting an ugly, boring bachelor townhouse when we got married, but I hated it and begged for us to buy our own house so I could make it beautiful. He wanted to make me happy, so we bought the best we could afford on his student-pastor salary: a little $60,000 ranch-style home that had new pink carpet and pink accents on the Formica countertops.

> No worries. I knew you have to look past some things in a house, right?

No worries. I knew you have to look past some things in a house, right? This house had a fireplace. Who cared about the color of the carpet?

Within a year of moving into our pink-carpeted house with the fireplace, Chad decided that he really wanted to be a teacher. He needed a graduate degree for that, so we found a one-year program at our alma mater, Columbia International University, and high-fived each other as we moved out of the house we just bought. We left the state with a For Sale sign in the yard. I'd watched my parents buy and sell houses, and I was confident our house would sell within a few months, no big deal — even though we hadn't lived there long enough to change the pink carpet and pink Formica counters.

3

This house was so tiny we had to remove the posters from our four-poster bed.

4

This house was so gigantic there were entire rooms that sat empty. I think God was just showing off with this place, making sure we knew he could provide whatever he wanted for us.

5

We brought our first baby boy home to this house. It was charming, but falling apart.

5

My mom helped me paint everything in this kitchen. Even the countertops. I'm sure the owners were thrilled.

6

We brought our second baby boy home to an apartment.

7

Finally, we bought our second house, where Baby Boy Number Three was born.

9

Our imperfect average dream house before.

9

Our imperfect average dream house after. I was sure we'd live here forever. I was wrong.

House 3: The Glorified Two-Car Garage

We were in our twenties when we made that move from Florida to South Carolina, so naturally we had no money and ate store-brand fish sticks for dinner and took out student loans to cover the tuition.

Did you catch that? We took out student loans so Chad could be a teacher. Let me make this perfectly clear: we borrowed money so we could secure a job making even less money than we had before. A foolproof plan.

We needed to rent a house while Chad was in school, since it was just a year-long program and we had a house for sale in another state. My criterion for finding a place to rent went as follows: find the least expensive place available that had a roof and a toilet. Is there a place where we can get paid to live? Take it. In the end, we paid $280 a month for a glorified two-car garage.

As the school year wore on, it was clear we didn't make enough to cover all of our expenses. We got behind on our house payment for the house in Florida that wasn't selling. By spring, we were getting threatening letters. Then we found out I was expecting.

By the end of the summer, Chad had finished the program and was looking for a teaching job. I was due in November. One of the first offers he received was a teaching position for $18,000 a year, with no insurance. Reality sets in fast when you have a house for sale, a baby on the way, and a handful of shiny new student loans.

House 4: The Two-Hundred-Year-Old Southern Mansion

We took the highest-paying teaching job Chad could find (it included insurance!) and moved to Macon, Georgia. The school hooked us up with a realtor, and we broke the news to her about our five-hundred-a-month housing budget. She got creative

11

The big rental house that was so not my style. We lived here for one year.

12

The rental that got foreclosed on. This was the move that broke the camel's back. I had enough.

13

Home. Because really, home is wherever you live with your people.

and connected us with the owners of a home she had been trying to sell for years. It was a 4,500-square-foot, *Gone with the Wind*–style home, complete with towering two-story columns and a gourmet kitchen. We could rent it for five hundred dollars a month while it was for sale, enough to cover a few expenses for the owners, who had pity on a poor young couple.

The house, a Greek Revival known in the National Register of Historic Places as the Randolph-Whittle House, was rich with historical significance. We had just moved out of a 250-square-foot garage into a mansion with a story. I was giddy. But within months of moving in and enduring a few showings, something miraculous happened: the house sold. The realtor thanked us, saying that having a couple live there probably helped the new buyers envision themselves there (even with most of the rooms empty).

I remember thinking how odd that was. Living in this couple's old house helped them sell it, yet we had our own house still for sale in Florida. My brain began collecting house-selling data.

House 5: The House in the Neighborhood with Bars on the Windows

Our little boy, Landis, was due to arrive in another month, so we scrambled to find a new place to live. Of course, I wanted a house, not an apartment. I love design, I love architecture, I love houses — I deserve a real house! Again, I searched for the least expensive place available.

I found a home built in 1910 with twelve-foot ceilings and five fireplaces that cost about the same rent per month as we paid in the mansion. When you are on a mission like this, you overlook the fact that neighboring homes have bars on the windows.

> We'd heard of the word *savings*, but it seemed like an urban myth.

I'll never forget our first day there. I had the screen door closed and the heavy wood door open when the mailman walked up on the porch. I stood there, nine months pregnant, and said hello. The mailman's response? He told me I should keep the door locked because the neighborhood wasn't safe. What had I done? It was the day we moved in and I already wanted to move out. Was this the life we were destined for? Moving from rental to rental, waiting for our house in Florida to sell?

We lived in the bars-on-the-windows neighborhood for six months, the amount of time on our lease. Our car was broken into, and I heard there was a vagrant living underneath the house next door. When there is a vagrant involved, you suddenly get excited about moving into a nice, new, clean, no-bars-on-the-windows apartment.

So that's how we had been married three years and had already lived in exactly five different homes. That's also how a person who thinks she is too good for an apartment can have a change of heart in a matter of months and become the most grateful person ever for not getting to live with five fireplaces after all.

House 6: The Apartment I Thought I Was Too Good For

So we moved into an apartment and I stayed at home with our son and we paid on our student loans and had no money. I repeat, *no money.* As in, I-couldn't-go-to-McDonald's-and-pay-for-a-small-order-of-fries no money. We'd heard of the word *savings,* but it seemed like an urban myth. I would go to the Dollar Store and look for the least expensive thing I could find just to enjoy having something new for our home. You know it's bad when you look for things on sale at the Dollar Store.

I wanted so badly to decorate, but we didn't have the means to spend anything on our house. The best I could do was to take down the rails that ran across the top of our four-poster bed to use as curtain rods in our bedroom. I felt hopeless. Tears were involved.

After three years on the market, our home in Florida finally sold. Lucky for us, we'd had renters for most of that time, but the relief of not owning that home was glorious. We sold it for exactly what we'd bought it for, so we had to sell one of our cars to pay the realtor's fee. You've never seen people so thrilled to sell their car.

After a year and a half of apartment living, Baby Boy Number Two, Cademon, was on his way. We had no plans, no goals, no hope of ever leaving the apartment. Chad was busy working at the school, and all I had to do every day was take care of a little boy, deal with a horrid case of morning sickness, and think about how I would be growing old in the apartment. We had major school debt, a little car payment, and a tiny bit of credit-card debt complete with not-so-perfect credit.

Then I started plotting. I wanted a house. I began to spend my days driving around town, studying neighborhoods. I also talked nonstop about buying a house. Poor Chad — I'm sure my discontentment was obvious.

We read Dave Ramsey's *Financial Peace* and within a year cleaned up our credit. We had learned the hard way about buying a house that wouldn't sell, so we had guidelines as we prepared for another move. I looked for a good deal, something we could sell easily when the time came. I looked for a house that I could immediately fix up with simple cosmetic changes like paint, changes that would make a big impact with little work. I looked for location more than anything else. Soon I narrowed our search down to a particular neighborhood. Maybe I wouldn't grow old in that apartment after all.

House 7: The Yellow House

We finally bought an adorable yellow 1940s mill house with 1,290 square feet. Perfect timing, because Baby Cade had arrived, and he was sleeping in a bassinet in the bathroom at the apartment. We paid $78,000 for our little yellow cottage. It didn't bother me that the washer and dryer were in the tiny kitchen or that there was no dishwasher. I could feel it: this house had good bones.

By then I knew it was best to make my house look good right away. I had learned that sometimes the unexpected happens and you move. I didn't know how long we would be there, but this time I was going to be prepared. I made the house pretty for me, and I made the house pretty in case we ever needed to sell it.

> I realized that making our house a *home* benefited our family in more ways than one.

When your first house sits on the market for three years, you do everything within your limited power to make sure you won't lose money on your next house. I thought of decorating as a job — a job I loved, a job we benefited from, and a job that I hoped would free us to sell if and when the time came.

Chad worked extra jobs in the summer months, so I was able to scrape together money to spend on the house. I painted walls and woodwork with wild abandon. I learned about plants and we had the prettiest front yard on the block. We put up a picket fence and I painted it white to complete the American Dream Look I was going for. I tried to create a simple, charming home with what we had.

In the meantime, Baby Boy Number Three, Gavin, was on the way. (We had found that out even before we moved, when Baby Cade was three months old.) Even though during our first months in our yellow house I was either sick or taking care of three little boys without the luxury of a dishwasher, I loved what I was doing.

In that little yellow house, I began to see that I was contributing to our family through decorating. I loved the fact that something I enjoyed was also worthwhile, both for the time we lived there and for the time we would sell.

I keep saying "I" not because my husband was asleep on the sofa with a bowl of chips balanced on his stomach but because he was working and coaching and didn't yet know the joy and payoff that creating a beautiful home could bring. It didn't bother me. I knew I had enough to do in the house that could keep me busy for years, so I focused on what I could do.

After eighteen months, Chad's side business took off. We decided to move to North Carolina to be closer to his family and my sister.

This time, I put a For Sale by Owner sign in the yard. Chad let me make some big decisions about selling the house, like figuring out the best way to advertise and choosing the asking price. Seeing those decisions turn out for the best gave me confidence in my house buying and selling skills. Within a week we got a cash offer for $20,000 more than what we had paid for the home just a year and a half earlier. We were shocked and thrilled.

This was a turning point for me. Having a house that took three years to sell was the best education I'd ever had. I realized that making our house a home benefited our family in more ways than one.

House 8: The Rental Where It Was Worth Losing Our Deposit

Whenever we move to a new city, we like to rent a house for a year before we buy so we can get a feel for what part of town suits us best. That's a lesson we learned the hard way from the house we bought in Florida. A few weeks before we moved to Greensboro, North Carolina, we narrowed our potential rentals down to two choices: a $1,200-a-month older ranch with wood paneling or a newer $1,300-a-month home. Always focused on money, I thought it would be wise to save a hundred dollars a month and live in the dark-paneled-family-room home.

After about two months of staring at that soul-sucking, dark paneling, I couldn't stand it any longer. I got busy priming and painting the paneling and the brick fireplace. Needless to say, at the end of our lease, the leasing company kept our $1,200 deposit.

The house actually looked good when we left. I knew that if I'd asked to paint, they would have said no, and that if I just went ahead and painted, they would most likely keep our deposit. It's not hard to do the math: if I had chosen the finished, cute, newer home, I wouldn't have had to paint and we would have paid exactly the same amount over the course of a year. But I hadn't known it would bother me so much to live in a dark-paneled home; it was depressing visually, emotionally, and even spiritually. Looking back, it was worth the $1,200 to get to know myself better.

House 9: Our Imperfect Average Dream House

A year after moving to North Carolina, we bought a charming 2,300-square-foot dream house. We had arrived! We had a lovely landscaped front yard and a flat back yard with actual trees. We had a dishwasher and two and a half bathrooms. And no dark paneling!

I envisioned years' worth of tweaking and painting and moving furniture and planting fun ahead of me in this home. Our boys were two, three, and six. Finally! We were settled. Just what I'd always wanted. Cue the white paint and tomato plants.

The house was my playground and Chad gave me free rein to make decorating decisions and learn from my mistakes. The house got a little prettier every day.

I didn't think our situation in that house could get any better. But it did. My sister and her husband and their twin baby girls moved in right around the corner, fourteen houses away. This, *this* was the life.

Meanwhile, Chad bought into a franchise. To me, we were rich. In truth, we were just average, but to be able to pay down our debt, buy tires if we needed them, and not worry about how much I spent at the grocery store was a luxury I'd never had in our eight years of marriage. Rich, I tell you! And that meant I could finally, at last, create the home I'd always wanted. I could join the club of women who loved their homes because they had the means to make them beautiful.

> The house was my playground and Chad gave me free rein to make decorating decisions and learn from my mistakes. The house got a little prettier every day.

Four years later, my visionary husband was ready for a change. The idea of his selling his franchise scared me. I liked not thinking about grocery money. I loved our life. I wanted to "finish" decorating. There was so much more to do. *No.*

But that winter, he sold his franchise. He made a good profit and had a job offer with a start-up company waiting for him. He encouraged me to have some work done on the outside of the house. That sounded like fun, so I had the outside painted and commissioned a new porch with a copper roof and a pair of wooden farmhouse doors.

By summer, the house was in its full glory. Every day, I'd see cars slow down to gaze at her beauty. I promise I'm not making this up. I even got my first design job from an impressed neighbor.

Unfortunately, while I was busy living my dream of fixing up our home even more, the company my husband worked for was busy going under. We needed a plan B. Fast.

We needed to sell the house. It was a painful decision. I teetered between crying uncontrollably and holding my chin high, claiming this was the greatest of adventures. I tried to look forward to getting to work on our next place. I took a ninety-minute class on how to sell your house by owner. I bought the most expensive ad in our local For Sale by Owner magazine, and within three weeks we had an offer.

We moved out of Our Imperfect Average Dream House on October 31, 2006. And I had a very real feeling that things were going to get worse before they got better.

House 10: The Free Two-Bedroom Condo

Miraculously, my sister's father-in-law heard about our situation, and out of his big heart he offered to let our family live rent-free in his two-bedroom condo that just happened to be empty. It was too good to be true. Free rent? We lived there

Come thou Fount of Every Blessing tune my Heart to sing thy Grace

HAND-LETTERED canvas by artist Lindsay Sherbondy, with a ceramic-boot umbrella stand turned into a vase, and a paperweight found for five dollars at a thrift store

for six hard months. It was the worst. It was horrible. It was the best. It was life changing. I'll tell you all about it in a later chapter, because this is where the good stuff happened.

Meanwhile, my husband decided to buy back into the original, successful franchise, but we had to find another city where the territory wasn't already owned by another franchisee.

House 11: The Big Rental House That Was So Not My Style

We moved to Charlotte in May of 2007 and brought with us about $150,000 of debt, including a new franchise, a truck for the franchise, my car, failed business debt, attorney fees, taxes, credit cards, school loans, a family loan, and medical bills. I don't know if I'm proud there were no nice vacations added to that mix or if I secretly wish there were. But I can promise, that debt wasn't for furniture.

During that time, I started a blog, mostly so I could leave comments at The Pioneer Woman's blog and have a link back to my own blog without feeling like an anonymous eighty-year-old killer. (That was back when I was pretty sure the internet consisted purely of terrorists and kidnappers.)

House 12: The Rental That Got Foreclosed On

A year later, the lease was up and we had found the part of town where we wanted to live. We moved to a less expensive rental in a small community. We still had six figures' worth of debt but were making huge payments, and it was nice to finally see the number quickly shrinking. Our credit was still suffering (again) and we were renting (again), but we had a plan and it seemed to be working.

We felt positive because Chad was so successful in the past with that same franchise. Did I mention it was in the car industry? We were together and had cheap rent and we were close to our church. We could finally pay off our debt and stay put for a while. Ahhh. *Now* I could feel settled. That was the summer of 2008.

People smarter than me refer to it as the Global Financial Crisis of 2008. Economists say it was the worst financial crisis since the Great Depression. All I know is that by the fall of 2008, things had changed, and the booming car industry that we had been so accustomed to for my husband's franchise dissipated. We were grateful for a job; so many people were losing theirs. But our plans to pay off our debt with lightning speed slowed to a crawl. We were happy simply to pay the rent on time.

Nine months into living in our cute little rental, the sheriff pulled up. She handed me a stack of papers with the homeowner's name at the top and the word *foreclosure* in bold. We had struggled to pay our rent on time every month, but we never missed a payment. We were never even late. It was early spring, and the house we were living in was being auctioned off in two months.

I was furious. Not at the owners but at God. How *dare* he? Did he not *know* that we had moved every year for the past three years? Did he not *know* that my boys needed stability? Did he not *know* that our credit was ruined and we needed to pay off debt and I could not even remember our zip code and I hated to move and I was exhausted and God, you are the one who created me with a love of being home and creating a beautiful home and all we've done is *move* around and I don't want to. *No.*

House 13: Home Because It's Where We Are

Naturally, it turned out to be the best possible thing that could have happened. I am so grateful. It just took awhile before I realized that. We found a rental through a friend and moved in a few weeks later.

It's been four years, and I love our rental home. I'm beyond content. I've embraced the fact that we are here, that this is one of the houses my boys will remember from their childhood, and that this is our home. For now.

> There's no magic signal to wait for. So I don't hesitate to hang things on the wall and make every room homey, because we never know when we might have to move again. No one really does.

I've learned that no one is going to give me special permission to make where I live home. There's no magic signal to wait for. So I don't hesitate to hang things on the wall and make every room homey, because we never know when we might have to move again. No one really does. Now on my thirteenth home, I've realized that home is wherever we are. I'm not going to waste time waiting for the next house we buy to create a beautiful place to live. I can't afford to wait until we have our life all perfectly organized and presentable to start enjoying it.

So here I am, sitting on my sofa in a rental house writing a book about creating a home. I used to think that renting made me unqualified to talk about home. Now I know it only qualifies me more.

Instead of wishing away years in past rentals and imperfect living situations, I wish I had simply embraced what was and made it lovely. For me. For my family. For now.

I know I'm not alone.

It was such a relief when I found an online community of women who, like me, weren't living in their dream houses. I've finally figured out that almost no one is living in their dream house. And I don't know anyone whose life has gone exactly

like they would have planned. You make the best choices you can at the time with the information you have, and then you deal with the consequences, and that's the part where your life happens. Every major decision we've made involved prayer and advice from wise people, but that was no guarantee that it would turn out the way I wanted, with a little white house and a picket fence.

Maybe you've moved too many times, or maybe you wish a move were in your future. Maybe you are renting and wish you weren't; maybe you are upside-down in a mortgage you don't want and can't move. Maybe you love where you are but feel like you aren't doing it justice with your decorating skills. Maybe you are waiting on that next house so you can finally start enjoying where you are.

The dream house isn't the answer.

The answer is a gift in disguise.

CHAPTER 3

Behind the Pretty Pictures

THE WORLD'S least expensive laundry-room makeover. We spent $175 on shelves, a counter, a quart of black paint, and a light fixture. And when we move, the light and counter can move with us.

*I fear a pristine life more than
I fear scuff marks on the floor.*

— DEBORAH NEEDLEMAN

Giving Up on Perfect
On Perfection and the Goal

No one has to teach us that perfect is the unofficial goal of American culture: we want straight A's, the perfect yard, and a tiny waistline. We've been duped into believing that flawless is the only acceptable outcome in every area of our lives. The media has bombarded us with Photoshopped, cellulite-free thighs and wrinkleless fifty-year-old actresses.

In 2004, Dove launched a Campaign for Real Beauty to help broaden the definition of beautiful among women. They created a video called "The Evolution of Beauty" that featured the fast-motion unnatural adjustments of a supermodel's face. After a crew attends to her makeup, hair, and lighting, the model is photographed and she looks great. But wait, it's time for the touch-ups, and we watch on the screen as her lips are digitally filled out, her neck is stretched and elongated (this is the point where every woman watching it suddenly sits up straight and stretches her neck up as high as possible), and her shoulders are manipulated and slimmed. It's not finished yet; they enlarge her eyes and hollow out her cheeks. The video ends with haunting words on a black screen: "No wonder our perception of beauty is distorted."

I didn't know whether to be happy that even models are heavily Photoshopped, or mad that even models are heavily Photoshopped. Either way, I felt tricked and a little dumb for comparing myself with models. Even models don't look like models.

It's crazy to compare ourselves with women in advertisements. And it's crazy to compare our homes with photos we see in magazines and online. It takes only a second to cross over from enjoying pretty pictures to contrasting our homes with them, and suddenly we feel as if we live in a frat house run by blind circus clowns from 1970s Vegas.

The purpose of these photos is to inspire, but well-staged pictures can sometimes leave us feeling hopeless, frustrated, and even ashamed of how we live. Why do we compare our everyday homes with homes featured in magazines? Why can't we see the beauty in both? If we feel bad after looking at a pretty photo, then we are looking at it all wrong.

It's Not the Photo's Fault

I'm a devoted fan of shelter and home magazines. I've loved them from a young age, and because I am nothing but selfless and my goals are always to help better the world, one of my childhood dreams has been to be featured in a magazine. You know, an aspiration right up there with curing disease and protecting peace and things of that nature.

Well, that dream came true. Our home has been featured in both *Better Homes and Gardens' Do It Yourself Magazine* and their *Christmas Ideas* issue, as well as in *Cottages and Bungalows* magazine, and my office was featured in *Ladies' Home Journal*. So it's official; the magazines have run out of perfect homes to photograph.

And what do we all think when we see a beautiful photo in a magazine? "Gosh, that [insert room you are looking at] is so clean. My [same type of room] looks like a disaster compared with that. I am a filthy slob. And that room is so pretty. How does she do it? I must be doing it all wrong because my [room that I now hate] doesn't look like that. Forget it. I give up."

Even though we all *know* that no real home looks perfect in its natural state, we still compare our everyday homes with those touched-up, cleaned-up, prettied-up photos.

Of course, we wouldn't dare compare the photo we snapped of ourselves with our phone in the carpool line with our neighbor's wedding portrait. Those are two very different events, right? A bride hires the best photographer she can afford, pays to get her makeup done, wears a gown she's dreamed about all of her life, picks the one best photo out of dozens, and then the photo is touched up, lightened up, blown up, and framed up in a frame handpicked to complement the lace on the gown. The purpose of a wedding portrait is to capture the bride on her once-in-a-lifetime special day. No one would accuse her of trying to show off and make us all feel bad. We don't look at a wedding photo and feel ashamed that we aren't forever walking around with an updo and heels. Looking like a bride every day is not our goal.

It's the same with photos of homes in magazines. Every layout you see had smart editors, highly trained photographers, thoughtfully placed accessories, manufactured light, and a team of people choosing the best angle. All of that was done to inspire and motivate us, as a gift, not to shame us. The everyday messes are in a closet or a corner just out of view of the camera. And the extra props are all on the floor, and after the editors and photographers and art director are finished, everyone takes a few minutes to put the house back together, because magazine photo shooting is messy business.

The second I was done snapping photos of my office for *Ladies' Home Journal*, I took that round tray off my desk to make room for a trusty pile of junk so I could relax and get some work done. It would be a tragedy if my office always looked clean. Just like it would be tragic if we thought we had to live our lives with our hair in a perfectly messy bun while wearing a wedding gown and a hurty pair of heels. It's hard to be creative in an office that can never look messy. That's not its purpose. And it's impossible to snuggle with your sick baby on the sofa in a wedding gown and hurty heels.

BEFORE My office, cleaned up for its photo shoot

AFTER My office the way it usually looks

A GALLERY WALL of random items looks great because it's all wood and black and white. But what really makes this space cozy is the dog on the sofa.

As readers and consumers, we get to choose how we use these photos. When we allow them to shame us, that's our choice. And we miss the inspiration they offer.

The same goes for do it yourself (DIY) home and craft blogs. They are written by talented women and are full of motivating ideas that almost anyone can do. DIY blogs have inspired me to create more beauty in my home, and I like to think that I've contributed to the DIY community with my own blog.

The only problem is you can't DIY yourself into loving your home. No amount of painted furniture or stenciled pillows will make you more content with what you have.

Creating a beautiful project may bring temporary satisfaction, but unless you look at your home through the right lens, you'll quickly wonder why you're still annoyed with your space.

Consider these questions:

- Do you walk slowly through Anthropologie or Pottery Barn and look longingly at the tablescapes and pillows and touch the displays and then walk out overwhelmed and empty-handed?
- Do you linger at a flea market that's full of beautiful one-of-a-kind treasures, but can't make a decision, and so somehow you end up buying what everyone else has, and then wonder why you don't like your home?
- Do you have a stack of the latest design books and shelter magazines but still have no idea where to start?
- Are you worried you won't decorate the "right" way? Worried that everyone will know that you have no idea what you are doing?
- Are you newly married with more time than money or an empty nester with more money than time, and are ready and willing to invest your limited resources, but you're afraid it will all be wasted?
- Are you struggling with indecision and lack of motivation (and by that, I mean have you had paint samples taped to your wall for more than a month)?

I've lived almost all of those scenarios. But creating a beautiful home doesn't have to be so difficult. It's decorating, not dental hygiene. It's supposed to be fun! (My apologies to all the dental hygienists; I'm sure you find your jobs to be really fun.)

"Come to me, all of you who are tired from carrying heavy loads, and I will give you rest."
— MATTHEW 11:28

As women, we ache to believe that real beauty can be found in the midst of imperfection. We are crying out for permission to lower our standards.

Let yourself know: permission granted.

What if there were a middle ground between a magazine-ready room and a neglected room? What if you created a home that is welcoming and works for your family? What if you looked to trends for ideas but believed it's okay to use what is beautiful and functional for *you*?

What if your house were patiently waiting to be enjoyed?

Done Is Better Than Perfect

A friend told me once that she and her husband didn't like the color of their bathroom but didn't want to repaint it because it was too much work. I asked what part of it was so hard, and she said, "Removing the toilet." Insert the loud noise of a record scratching while the earth's rotation grinds to a halt and every human stops what they are doing and looks our way. "What? You said you wanted to paint the bathroom, right? Not renovate."

"Yeah, but my parents recently painted their bathroom and they took the toilet out. Otherwise how would they paint the wall all the way behind it?"

This is what perfection does to us. We put off doing all sorts of fun things because to do them perfectly would be entirely too much work. So instead of having a slightly imperfect finished space with a few unpainted inches behind a permanent toilet that no person will ever see, we have a space we hate.

I use this example because most of us have moved past this scenario. Most of us would be okay feeling we didn't need to paint every square inch behind the toilet. If you can't get to it with a tiny brush, then our eyes probably can't get to it either. Don't throw the baby out with the bathwater. Or toilet water, in this case.

When it comes to perfection you have two choices:

1. Work really hard to attain it.
2. Give up.

Many of us have tried the first way. We've worked ourselves (or our poor husbands) to the weary bone trying to measure up to an unrealistic goal. We've either failed or are still wasting precious time chasing perfection. We overbuy, overspend, overdecorate, and overfret. We have a cute, somewhat organized hoard of home accessories tightly packed away in the closets. We are constantly trying the next DIY craze in our homes only to find that we still feel discontented when we look around our rooms.

Others of us have just given up. Sometimes giving up looks like using hand-me-down furniture that isn't serving your family well because you are so worried about making a bad decision. You have stacks of framed photos behind the sofa for fear of making an extra nail hole. You throw in the ugly towel from

your former roommate because buying new towels is overwhelming. You've given up on the dream of ever having a home you love.

Sometimes giving up looks like having an almost empty house. You don't know what to purchase for your home and family, so you purchase nothing.

Winston Churchill said, "The maxim 'Nothing prevails but perfection' may be spelled *paralysis*." It's just too difficult to make the perfect decision about a sofa. Let me tell you why: the perfect decision about a perfect sofa doesn't exist.

Whether we work too hard or just give up, both tendencies stem from one main issue: we've allowed the myth of perfection to take our minds hostage. We want perfection, and we want it yesternow.

Giving Up on Perfect

Instead of giving up on a perfect idea, what if you gave up on perfection? Go ahead: pick the sofa that is super comfy, knowing that in five years it will have a stain on it and not look brand new. Lower your expectations and realize that as long as we all choose to walk around clothed, the laundry will never really be finished. If we live fully in a home, there will be messes. Why does that surprise us and make us feel guilty? As long as we eat, walk, and need places to sit down, the kitchen sink will have a few dirty dishes in it and the living room will never be clutter-free for long.

> I realized that making our house a *home* benefited our family in more ways than one.

Giving up is the first step to creating the home you love. The goal of perfection does nothing but hold you back. Giving up on trying to have the perfect house is a form of rest. In her book *Choosing Rest*, Sally Breedlove says, "We find rest in the incompleteness of the present moment as we learn to recognize the goodness of what is and we trust that what is needed for the future will be added at the proper time."

Allowing things in our homes and in our lives to be incomplete, imperfect, and undone in some ways is a form of trust. Can you give up and allow some imperfections in your life?

We get stuck in this way of thinking:

- I want to like my house, therefore I shall change it until I like it.
- I want to like my body, therefore I shall change it until I like it.
- I want to like my life, therefore I shall change it until I like it.

Instead of focusing on this way of thinking, what if you changed what you like?

Yes, we can change things in our lives, but we often work hard for change only to figure out that having a pretty room, body, or bank account isn't all it was cracked up to be.

50

FOCUS on the beauty that's there,
not the imperfect and undone

It's the same with having the goal of a less messy house. You can learn tips and tricks to help keep your home more put-together and beautiful. Or you can accept the fact that your home will be imperfect and that each season of your family's life will bring different kinds of beautiful messes.

But here's the real secret. What if you did both? What if you were less hard on yourself for the ways you and your home fail, and you looked instead at what's already there? What if creating a beautiful home was less about stuff and more about attitude? What if you already have everything you need to have the home you've always wanted?

You don't have to get perfect to have a pretty house. Most of us simply need to learn to see the beauty in the imperfect. Because life is gloriously messy. We can find rest in our less than perfect circumstances when we figure out that no amount of striving can create the perfect life we think we are looking for. True rest comes when we realize that we can't get it from trying extra hard. We find rest when we give up.

CHAPTER 4

Signs of Life

Don't scrub the soul out of your home.

— MARY RANDOLPH CARTER

The Gift of Messes, Mistakes, and Other Beautiful Imperfections

I wish I had given myself permission to lower my high standards in those early years of my marriage when I was caught up in what my houses were lacking. Because the irony is that giving up on perfection isn't a failure. It's a gift.

The Freedom of Imperfections

Nine years ago, we paid cash for a well-made, super-comfy sofa. I love that sofa. But a few years ago, I noticed that the edges were starting to wear dangerously thin and the fabric was stained and fading. I should have known better than to make fun of people who use those grandma arm-cover protectors. I bet their sofa arms look pristine. I even got a little teary-eyed knowing how much we enjoyed that sofa and also knowing that we couldn't afford a new one. Deep in my twisted thoughts, I asked myself why, *why* was I such a fool to allow my sofa to be used so carelessly?

But there is a good side to having a not-so-perfect sofa. I can freely have friends over, friends with toddlers who eat melty chocolate-chip cookies on the sofa, friends who don't gasp in horror when a liquefied chip falls onto the fabric. And now when one of my boys isn't feeling too well and there is a threat of his you-know-whatting his Spaghettios, I let him rest on the sofa on a blanket of towels without fear that anything will be ruined. My husband can plop down in his favorite spot, and if his greasy popcorny hands happen to fall onto the arm of my precious sofa, I'm not tempted to shoot him down with a disapproving look.

In fact, the only thing worse than a falling-apart, used-up, five-year-old sofa is a perfectly pristine five-year-old sofa. Not only do I think our sofa is thrilled to be fulfilling its sofa-y purpose, but we are much more free to enjoy it because of its imperfections. And I've since slipcovered it in white, so now we can fully enjoy it and it can be bleached clean — the best of both worlds.

It's easy to make decisions based on what others will think, settling for the appearance of perfection instead of insisting on authenticity. But is that really how we want to live? Just keeping up appearances?

Homes are happiest when they are being used. Sofas are meant to be sat on, chairs are made to be pulled around when needed, favorite items are meant to be displayed. Have you ever walked into a model home? It is eerily perfect. You can tell right away that no one lives there. I always get the feeling that a robot wearing an apron and a cheap wig is standing just around the corner. It is not a real home because *life* happens in real homes. So real homes should have signs of life.

The Role of Imperfections

Years ago I had a friend who seemed to have it all together. I mean, we all know that nobody's perfect, but every now and then we meet someone who tests the theory. She was breathtakingly beautiful — like, for real. She was the prettiest friend I've ever had, her husband had a fantastic stable job, and their two children were darling. Her house was gorgeous. She never seemed to have to work on it; it just *was*. She was also one of the kindest people I knew. Drat!

But I always felt uncomfortable around her, as if I wasn't good enough. Being around someone who seems perfect only makes our own imperfections more glaring.

Then my friend and I got to know each other more. She shared some issues she was struggling with, and a funny thing happened. I started to feel comfortable around her. I finally figured out that we were both members of the same club. Human, imperfect, and lovely. I could relax, be myself, and not feel judged, because we were both aware of our flaws. Sharing the not-so-pretty parts of our lives solidified our friendship.

That is how it is with your home. The imperfections play an important role: they put people at ease.

When I walk into a house, my eyes immediately dart around hoping to find something imperfect so that I can know this is a house where I can be real.

The truth is I'm just not comfortable in a house that seems perfect. I get distracted and start thinking all about myself. I wonder if I can move this pillow to sit down. I'd better have water to drink instead of wine in case I spill it. Instead of enjoying the company of the hostess, I worry about how to act in the presence of a person who seems to have it all together. I wonder what she must think of me and the mess that I am when her house is so beautiful.

It finally dawned on me that if I'm not able to let my guard down in a perfect house, maybe others feel the same way. And if other people feel that way, why the heck was I working so hard to make our home appear to be perfect? True, I want our home to be welcoming. I want it to be comfortable. But welcoming and comfortable do not have to equal perfection. I was doing it all wrong. Imperfections aren't bad after all. They are even valuable.

Think about it: what makes marble and granite so desirable? They are real, from the earth, one of a kind. Imperfect, each with unique markings and move- ment. They have a high value because each piece is different, rare, and we find beauty in their subtle organic nature. It's the same thing with wood. The imper- fections prove its authenticity. Genuine high-end leathers usually have a tag informing the buyer that imperfections are to be expected, because it's the real thing.

A few years ago I needed a pair of lamps. I'm pretty patient when it comes to waiting for the right thing to purchase. But after months of keeping my eye out for some, I started to get restless. Finally, a light from heaven shone down

HOMES are happiest when they are being used.

on a pair of perfectly shaped large white gourd lamps from HomeGoods. I knew they were the right lamps for me.

When I picked one up, I noticed that the base was cracked. I asked the clerk if they could mark it down, and he said yes, but he warned me not to buy the lamp, because it was broken. I could see that all I needed to do was turn the lamp around and it would look just like its twin. Also, I've learned that buying something already imperfect is a bonus. In my house, most things are tested for sturdiness within one hour to fourteen days of arriving. So bringing in something that was already broken but still looked good meant that was one less thing I needed to worry about.

I bought the lamps. I secured the broken one with a layer of superglue around the cracks. It's still broken, but it works great. I didn't get in trouble. No one laughed. The decorating police didn't give me a citation on cute expensive paper. The lamps look lovely together. Store Clerk: 0, Imperfectionists: 1.

What if you welcomed people into the mess, the lacking, and the undone? Imperfections bear witness to the fact that we are normal, approachable, real people. Why try to hide that?

I know what you're thinking. Is she trying to tell us that we should all be slobs? Do we stop making our beds and brushing our teeth and mowing the grass? Do I have to go out and buy a broken lamp too?

In her book *The Reluctant Entertainer*, Sandy Coughlin writes, "Excellence is working toward an attainable goal that benefits everyone, while perfection comes from a place of great need — usually the need to avoid criticism and gain praise and approval from others." We like to tell ourselves that we are insisting on perfection for the betterment of those around us. But really, insisting on perfection is a self-centered act.

Here's the thing: if you're reading this, you're probably not in danger of going overboard with imperfection. Irresponsible people aren't reading a book about imperfection; they are too busy programming their reality TV schedule and not cleaning out their refrigerator.

Most of us have the utmost respect for responsibility, with perfectionist thoughts whispering in our ears all the time. Most of us need permission to let a few things slide.

So if your teeth are falling out and your grass is knee high, then you probably don't need to hear that imperfections can be a good thing. You have permission to stop reading this book and use it as a paperweight for all of the magazines you refuse to throw out. But if you are overwhelmed with expectations and comparisons and keeping up with people you don't even like, maybe it's time to embrace the not so perfect.

It's Time to Stop Apologizing

As I entered the home of a friend, two things were obvious: the owner had impeccable taste, and she had the budget to back it up. But I was welcomed with an apology for "what a mess" her house was. That secretly made me happy. Not only did she know how to create a beautiful home, she must also know how to live beautifully within the mayhem. I started scanning for the mess. Nothing caught my eye, but she pointed things out: "Oh, just ignore that window, we've been meaning to get new drapes." "I've been trying to get my husband to paint that wall forever." "I'm so sorry, those pillows just don't look right on our old sofa."

After the tour, she covered everything with a shocking statement. "I'm so embarrassed. This house is such a mess." Every time someone came to the door for our gathering, she welcomed her with an apology, making sure to point out every flaw (I still couldn't find any) so the guest was sure to know that *she* knew her home was less than perfect.

> Imperfections bear witness to the fact that we are normal, approachable, real people.

All I could think was that if this beautiful, well-appointed home wasn't good enough for her, then my ramshackle, motley house certainly would never be okay. I made a mental note never to invite her over. No matter what.

I had fallen into the apology trap myself, of course. I always apologized for my home to protect myself so people wouldn't think I was a slob, or at least so they

For Renters, Transients, and Modern-Day Nomads

Renting with Purpose

I remember so clearly more than fifteen years ago when I was a stay-at-home mom with a new baby boy living in The Apartment I Thought I Was Too Good For while we were living on just Chad's income. Another mom with a newborn, a full-time job, and a pretty house said to me, "You are so lucky. I wish I could stay home with our baby." I remember thinking, *But I think you're lucky because you bought a house.* And then I realized that she called *me* lucky.

Most of us renters are choosing to live someplace we don't love because there are more important things we need to tend to: raising children, paying off debt, living close to family, finding a job, supporting a spouse, being independent, being financially responsible. Remember, there are a lot of women who would consider you lucky that you even got to make that choice in the first place.

You will look back and have fond memories of the rental you currently despise. And choosing a less than ideal home in order to have the kind of home life, financial peace, or family circumstance you want is not the kind of decision you look back on and regret. Remind yourself that you are being intentional. Choosing to rent just might be a gift after all.

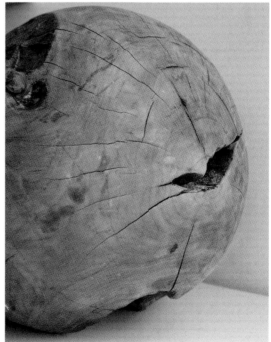

IMPERFECTIONS put people at ease.

would know that I acknowledge I can be a slob and that I'm not okay with it and that really I have much higher standards than this and my house does not meet my requirements. But that day, I realized that when I apologize for my home, I'm declaring to all within earshot that I'm not content. That I'm silently keeping score. That I put great importance on the appearance of my home and maybe, just maybe, I'm doing that when I visit your home too.

One time I took my apologies too far and went on and on about how a big beautiful home we were renting (The Big Rental House That Was So Not My Style) was so, well, *not* my style. My guest quietly commented that she would love to live in my house. I'm so glad she said that, because it made me realize what I was really doing: being ungrateful.

Don't apologize for what you have. It makes guests feel uncomfortable, it encourages discontentment, and if you're married and your husband hears you apologizing for what he's provided, it could be hurtful.

Years have passed since I visited that apologizing friend. If we still lived in the same town, I'd have no problem inviting her over. She might not even notice what a hot mess my house is; people caught up in perfection are usually much harder on themselves than they are on others. And if she did notice, maybe the fact that I'm okay with it would be freeing to her. No apologies necessary.

Imperfection Is a Sign of Maturity

In her book *Sink Reflections*, Marla Cilley, also known as The FlyLady, says, "House-keeping done incorrectly still blesses the family." It's the same with creating a beautiful home. Decorating done incorrectly still blesses the family. And decorating done good enough is prettier than decorating not done at all.

Of course, some things in life — taxes, flying a plane, heart surgery, dialing 911 — need to be done as close to perfectly as possible. But other things — killing a spider, washing your face, buying an area rug — just need to be done. Whether it's saving money, cleaning the house, brushing your teeth, or picking a paint color, doing these things is still worth it even if they aren't done to absolute perfection. At times, good enough and done is a smarter choice than perfect, and simply making a choice is often a sign of maturity, balance, and contentment.

Once we realize that the goal is not having a perfect home, we can create a beautiful home out of freedom instead of fear. Instead of seeing a used-up sofa with a little rip, we see a loved-on piece of our story, a cushy place that has faithfully held the heinies of friends through joys and sorrows. Sure, we may still need or want a new sofa, but instead of making a choice out of dislike for what we have, we make a choice out of gratitude.

> Instead of seeing imperfections as thorns in my decorating flesh, I want to open my eyes and see them as signs of life.

A pile of dirty shoes in not-quite-grown-man sizes is a sign of recent adventures. The broken chair leg propped up with a stack of books is a reminder that we could have spent cash on a new chair but decided to spend it on something more important right now. The too-small twin bed in the fifteen-year-old's room could be a trigger to be annoyed that we have to provide a new bed, maybe even a bigger room. Or it could be a time to appreciate that our boys are growing up, which is exactly what they should be doing. What a gift.

Instead of seeing imperfections as thorns in my decorating flesh, I want to open my eyes and see them as signs of life. These messes all stem from gifts in my life. I still clean the mud off shoes (or make my boys do it), but I also know that if a neighbor walked in and saw a trail of mud, I wouldn't need to be embarrassed. It's just proof of lives being lived, and houses are for living. My home is a reflection of our life, and life's messes can be gloriously beautiful.

CHAPTER 5

A Place of Peace

FEET ON THE TABLE, pillows
spread around—this room was
created to be lived in.

He is happiest, be he king or peasant,
who finds peace in his home.

— JOHANN WOLFGANG VON GOETHE

Embracing the True Purpose of Your Home

Before you start making changes to create a beautiful, imperfect home, you need to define your home's purpose. This is part of putting on new lenses as you look around your house. How do you want people to feel when they come over? How do you want your family to feel about the home they live in?

Think about words you would use to describe the feel of the home you've always wanted, and don't read on until you have a few descriptive words in your head.

I asked this question on my blog, Nesting Place. Here are the results of an unscientific poll (meaning I sat in my pj's with my iced coffee and made a note of which words were repeated) of the ever-brilliant, ever-purposeful Nesting Place readers:

- ☐ Relaxed
- ☐ Restful
- ☐ Real
- ☐ Welcoming
- ☐ Inspiring
- ☐ Simple
- ☐ Comfortable
- ☐ Cozy
- ☐ Safe
- ☐ Accepting
- ☐ Peaceful
- ☐ Nurturing
- ☐ Family oriented
- ☐ Fun
- ☐ Timeless
- ☐ Sanctuary
- ☐ Joyful

Did you think of some of the same words? Or similar ones? You may have additional words, but hardly anyone would say, "Well, I like a safe home, but I certainly wouldn't ever want my home to be considered fun." No one ever says they want their home to feel unwelcoming. Or cold or unfriendly or unaccepting or harsh or lifeless or stressful.

The descriptions that readers listed are the words we want our homes to whisper in the ears of our family and friends. This is the type of home we all long for.

Use these words to remind you of the real purpose of your home as you make it into a place that suits your family. There's no right or wrong answer for the purpose of your home; *you* get to decide.

You might be thinking, *Those are real nice words, lady, but how does that affect how my house looks today? I have an empty room, woman, HELP!* Trust me. Those words can help you take the next step in creating the home you've always wanted, and we're going to find out how.

A Place of Beauty and Creativity

One of my top priorities for my home is for it to be a place of beauty. Notice I didn't say I want my home to be perfect. Also, I really don't care for it to be expensive. Beauty is something altogether different. I've yet to meet a woman who wants her home to be ugly. Enjoying beautiful things is part of being human. It is how God made us.

Isn't home the safest place to begin coming alive to the creativity we all possess?

How to Create Intentional Spaces

A place to connect.

If I want my home to be a place of connection, I'll ask genuine questions and get to know the people in my home. I'll prioritize good conversation and be sure I have adequate, comfortable seating so people will stick around.

A safe place to make mistakes.

If I want my home to be a safe place to make mistakes, I'll lower my standards for myself first, be forgiving of my own mistakes, and allow others to see me laughing at myself. I'll display and use the imperfect in my home. That spelling test where he made a C but did his best? On the fridge. The frame with the broken glass? Put it on the wall; it still looks great. The leather chair with the rips? It's loved and used daily. I don't point out and apologize for those imperfections. I embrace, love, and enjoy them.

A place of inspiration.

If I want my home to be inspiring, I'll pay attention to what inspires me. I'll collect inspiring mementos and show them off unashamed, regardless of the trends.

A place of authenticity.

If I want my home to be real, I'll learn to embrace the imperfect, find the beauty in the undone, the haphazard, the unkempt, the everydayness, and the mess. I'll find the beauty in what is. I'll accept that the messes unique to my home are a sign of a full and beautiful season of life.

A place of comfort.

If I want my home to be comfortable, I'll stop apologizing and focus on others instead of on myself by creating a home that serves people, not a place where people serve and protect our fancy stuff.

A place of rest.

If I want my home to be a place of rest, I'll consider my attitude and the tone I set when I am home. I'll practice resting in the midst of the undone, even if that means letting the dirty dishes sit so I can laugh with a friend who stopped by.

A place of joy.

If I want my home to be joyful, I'll surround myself with people and places and memories that remind me of good times. I'll remove items that bring back sad memories or that I dislike and surround myself with items that bring me joy.

A place of contentment.

If I want my home to be a place of contentment, I'll practice gratitude in my home. I'll say out loud things in my home that I'm thankful for instead of dwelling on what I think is missing.

Here's an example of how knowing the purpose of your home helps you make wise, and freeing, decorating decisions.

One of the uses of our family room is to seat a crowd of people somewhat comfortably. We host a weekly community group, I had a big book-signing party for my sister, I've hosted craft days, and we usually have two large family Christmas gatherings at our house; we even had my husband's ordination in our home. So one of the things I've challenged myself to do is to have as much seating as I can possibly squeeze into the room without making it look like a waiting room in a doctor's office.

From time to time, I'll look around and count the number of easily accessible seats that a heinie could fill if need be. It's a game I play with myself (clearly I'm the life of any party), and then I try to beat my own record to see what kind of creative seating I can tuck into a corner or under a table.

Here's the breakdown of the points system:

The sectional = 5
Two upholstered chairs = 2
Two pairs of side chairs, upholstered but not super cozy = 4

I bought two pairs of side chairs specifically to add more seating. I didn't need the chairs to complete the design-y look I was after. I actually had to get creative to fit them in. One pair flanks a dresser; the other pair sits at the game table. And if we really need to, I can pull in a pair of parsons chairs from the adjoining breakfast area.

On any given day, without moving a thing, I can manage to fit seating for eleven in our family room. Thirteen if you count the bar stools. Fifteen if you move in the cushy end chairs from the breakfast table. That doesn't even count the other four chairs at the table. I make it all work because I know that one of the purposes of our home is to make large groups of people feel welcome and comfortable.

TOP A pair of velvet chairs I lovingly call "the copper twins," picked up at the Salvation Army for forty dollars each

My friend Darlene created a Master Designer Manifesto:

I am a Master Designer.

I love beauty;
I see potential and I want to fill it with beauty. I aim to create something beautiful that is worthy of joy.

Design is a high calling,
one that can improve the lives of others, be a means to foster relationships, and add much joy to my family.

I appreciate fine and lovely things,
but they are not my treasures. I know what is truly important, and I do not aim to "store up my treasures here on earth."

I live to bring glory to God, the ultimate master designer.
He created beauty. He created all beautiful things. And he created my passion for beauty and set that joy in my heart.

Everything that I create, and have created,
is because I myself was created by a master. I am a master designer.

—*Darlene Weir, FieldstoneHillDesign.com*

My sister, Emily, wrote a book called *A Million Little Ways* about the connection between art and how God created us, and what that means in our daily lives. She writes, "In the beginning, God made art ... The first thing we know about God is he made art ... What is the first thing we know about people? We were made in his image ... You are art and you make art."

It shouldn't surprise or shame us that we are drawn to surrounding ourselves with beauty.

Last summer, I traveled to Tanzania. I'll tell you more about that in a later chapter, but I mention it here because of what that trip taught me about our call to beauty and creativity. I knew we were going to be visiting poverty-stricken areas, and I wondered whether I would still see signs of creativity there. Surely art is a luxury?

Then I met a Maasai woman wearing a large beaded necklace. Through the translator, I told her how much I admired it and asked how long it took her to make the necklace. Her answer was two weeks. Then she held her hand up signaling me to wait, walked inside her hut, and came back out with a necklace twice the size.

She was proud to show me her beautiful work. In the midst of poverty, famine, and everyday life in a mud hut, this woman made time for art.

I make art in my home because I was made in the image of my creator. I can't not do it. My home is my canvas. I am called to reveal the full glory of whatever home I'm in with whatever I'm given at that time. It's part of my love for beauty, a love we all have.

For instance, I'm a furniture tweaker. One of the ways I've learned I can make a change in my home for free is by moving furniture. That doesn't mean I'm not content. I know what discontentment looks like — an overall hopeless attitude, irresponsible shopping, and an ungrateful heart. But for me, moving furniture is just plain fun! It's a great way to exercise the creativity God has given me.

As a child, I dreamed of creating beautiful, meaningful rooms. Maybe you are one of those people too. Or maybe you'd just like to have a home where you are free to have people over and focus on them instead of all your home's imperfections.

Is your home just another place of unmet expectations, to-do lists, and exhaustion? Or is your home a haven, the safest place on earth, a place to come back to, a place to heal, a place to create, a place to risk and simply be? You get to decide.

Home On Purpose

What's the goal of your home? Maybe just for yourself or your family you could have a phrase that states the ultimate purpose of your home. Most of us have made goals for our lives and jobs and financial future, so why not for our houses or apartments, the places where we spend the majority of our lives?

The goal for our home is to be a place to connect with others, foster rest, inspire, and be a welcoming place to come back to. So even when my house is messy, I can see that my house is still meeting its true purpose. Wow! What a shift in my thoughts about my home. Suddenly, instead of focusing on what it isn't, I can focus on what it is.

I also know that while a cluttered house can be beautiful, an overly messy house doesn't usually meet my purpose for my home. So I try to keep it on the tidy side

BOTTOM Home; lived-in and loved-on.

Making a charmed and happy home
is a noble endeavor.

— DEBORAH NEEDLEMAN

without being too strict about it. (Of course, you and I and your mother-in-law all have different definitions of *messy*, but that's another book.)

Each season in our lives requires different services from our homes. If something isn't working for you, reevaluate. Right now, my husband is homeschooling our boys, and I run a business out of our home. Because of how we need our home to serve us, we changed an empty bonus room into a family room so we'd have a place for the menfolk to spread out books and dirty socks, and a quiet place for me to work and take pictures and create.

Knowing the true purpose of our home helps us make decisions like that. Decisions about moving, buying, or selling, about what to bring into our home, what to leave in our home, and what needs to go. Decisions like changing an unused dining room into a craft room, toy room, library, or office. Or changing an office back into a dining room. The home evolves as our needs change.

It's less about doing the "right" thing and more about creating a home that works for your family right now, a home that fulfills its purpose in this season. We have to remember this, because it can be easy to approach decorating in a way opposite to how we hope our home will feel. We make decisions as if we are being graded. We are paralyzed because we are afraid of being judged. We worry and procrastinate and waste years not enjoying where we live and making our family miserable as we whine and wish and verbalize our disappointment with our homes. (Not that I've ever done that or anything.) We treat our homes like checklists instead of canvases.

Look back at those words we listed earlier. The purpose of a home is less about stuff and more about people. The people who live there. The people who come there. Stuff can help us accomplish those goals, and we are going to talk about that too — it sure is hard to be cozy in a house with no furniture or blankets — but it is not the purpose of a home.

A home's greatest purpose is to serve people, not the other way around.

CHAPTER 6

Risk

SAILFISH I was a nervous wreck the day I bought my sailfish, but it was *so* worth the risk.

The dangers of life are infinite, and among them is safety.

— GOETHE

Take Some and Pass It On

After five years of running Nesting Place and helping friends, neighbors, family, and strangers with their homes, not to mention thirty-nine years of listening to my own backtalk in my head, I'm pretty sure I've figured out what most often holds us back from creating a beautiful, meaningful home on purpose.

It's not money.

It's not lack of creativity.

It's not that we don't have the time.

It's not that someone else is stopping us.

All those things come into play. But what is our biggest hurdle?

Fear.

We put off making decisions, hesitate to commit to a paint color, dream about trying that DIY project but worry we'd mess it all up. We assume that when others chose that bold color or bought that vintage sofa, it didn't feel like a risk to them. Since it feels scary to us, we stop. Or we take it to the other extreme. We put off buying that sofa that we've needed for three years and instead spend a small fortune buying too many tchotchkes, trinkets, set-arounds, and smalls because those are easy decisions.

Home is supposed to be the safest place on earth. We yearn to create that safe place for our family and guests. Yet we don't see our homes as safe places for us.

What if we looked at our homes not only as training grounds for our children to learn how to be responsible adults but also as training grounds for ourselves? What if we decided home was a safe place to make mistakes, take risks, play, and be who we want to be?

If you never did you should. These things are fun and fun is good.

Dr. Seuss

If we cannot be our true selves and make mistakes in our homes, how can we expect others to let their guard down while they are in our homes?

Everything important to you was a risk. It's a risk to go for the scholarship at your top choice university. It's a risk to say yes when he asks you to marry him. It's a risk to try out for the team, to push your creativity and then show it to people, to try a new recipe, to have children. Life is about taking risks, and risk-taking can be messy.

If you lower your expectations and decide that perfection isn't the goal, you'll be amazed at what you'll let yourself try.

The Nail Hole Diaries

I didn't realize until I started writing online how terrified some women (and many men) are of devaluing their homes by making a nail hole in the wall. Part of me wants to scream, "It's a ding-a-ling nail hole in the wall! Is there anything in life *less* risky than creating a one-millimeter hole in a wall that can be filled with your finger and some putty in two seconds?" A nail hole is the easiest repair. Wait, I don't even want to use the word repair because it insinuates it's a mistake. Filling a nail hole is the easiest tweak you can make in a home, next to changing a lightbulb. Nail holes are just part of living in a house. I'd say that a nail hole is the lowest entry-level risk-taking

We've Been Conditioned Not to Make Mistakes

Our (Risky) Room

Putting duct tape on our walls: **risk**

Buying a rug online: **risk**

Hanging sheets on our windows: **risk**

Buying a chair from the thrift store without knowing where it will go: **risk**

Painting said chair even though it was "good wood": **risk**

Hanging a salvaged oversized lantern: **risk**

Painting the walls in a rental: **risk**

Having a room we love to be in:

totally worth the risk — priceless

ABOVE RIGHT Bedroom painted gray with white duct tape creating a patterned wall

BELOW RIGHT One of the many phases of our gallery wall.

action you could have in life, other than getting no whip on your coffee.

Part of me also understands the hesitancy to take a first step toward anything we are unsure about. I talk big when it comes to making nail holes, but get me in the makeup department of a store and I feel like a seven-year-old. A seven-year-old boy. I have no idea what I'm doing when it comes to cosmetics. To me, cosmetics are risky, so I avoid them even though I love the idea of using them well.

But back to nail holes. I have a gallery wall in my living room, and it takes awhile to get pictures where I want them. I recently counted all the nail holes in that wall.

There were eighty-three. Sue me. *Eighty-three nail holes* on one wall, and no one came and arrested me and put me in fabric-lined designer handcuffs.

To make a point on my blog (nail holes have become quite the topic of conversation there), I timed myself to see how long it would take to repair those eighty-three nail holes. It took me six minutes to fill them and three minutes to sand them after the filler stuff dried.

I have zero regret for making so many holes as I played around with my gallery wall. Sometimes you have to make something imperfect before you can make it pretty. Can I get an amen?

So please, for the love of all that is lovely, don't be afraid to make a nail hole. Just make the hole, hang the art, I beg of you. If you have never made a nail hole, get up right now, find a nail and a hammer (or a shoe or a rock will do) and make a hole in your wall. It will instantly free you. If you have *major* nail-hole-in-the-wall issues, start with making a nail hole in your closet. You must move past your nail-hole fears in order to create a beautiful home. This is not optional.

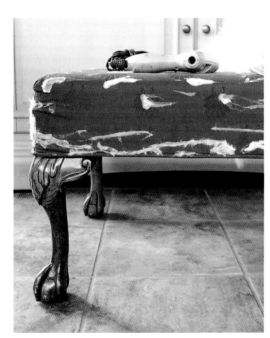

FIVE-DOLLAR yard-sale ottoman, plus twelve dollars' worth of pretend fur secured with hot glue equals one sassy footstool. You can't ruin something you didn't like in the first place.

82

THIS HUTCH started out black. I painted over it and then made a book page garland for a temporary party decoration. I loved it so much it has stayed up for two years.

The thing is having a home you love *always* starts with making it imperfect. Ironic, isn't it? You can't be afraid to paint your walls because you might get paint on your walls. That's the whole idea. It starts with taking a little risk so you can build to the bigger risks. You can do this.

"You Can't Do That"

Risks don't have to be big projects. Maybe for you a risk is finally moving the sofa to the other wall to see how it looks. Maybe a risk is going to HomeGoods and purchasing four new pillows in bold colors, leaving the tags on and putting them on the sofa simply to see if one of those colors works. Only you know what is risky for you in your home.

But all of us need practice to feel better about taking risks. My favorite things in my home are all results of taking a risk, and the things that didn't work out were also results of risk. Having the things I love was worth the risk of trying some things that didn't turn out.

Some risks that turned out in disaster:

- I had a pretty oval mirror in my office and wanted to see what it would look like in the boys' room, so I set it on the dresser, leaning it against the wall instead of hanging it. I didn't want to make needless nail holes. I figured I'd give it a day or two to see if I liked it. A week later, I heard a huge crash, and to my surprise the mirror had fallen off the dresser and onto the floor, cracked into pieces. It was irreparable. I had forgotten about it.
- I bought a pair of lamps from a thrift store, but one didn't work. No problem, I just Googled how to rewire a lamp. After shocking myself, I learned how to pay closer attention to the wires.
- Last year, I was sure that moving our two youngest boys into the bonus room would solve all of our room-sharing issues. We spent the entire day taking apart beds and moving two rooms of stuff all over the house. Turns out not having a closet in a boys bedroom is more detrimental than I thought. Six months later, we spent another whole day moving everything back the way it was.

I don't regret any of those risks. Why? Because if I hadn't tried changing it up, I'd still be sitting here wondering how it would have turned out.

Here's another scenario I see all the time. You've watched your friends or DIY bloggers find yard-sale pieces and then paint them. So you buy an eight-dollar wood table at a yard sale. You bring it home, and naturally, it sits in the garage for six months. Finally, you decide to paint it. Your husband asks you what you are doing, and you say you are going to paint the eight-dollar yard-sale table that's been sitting in the garage for six months. His reply? "You shouldn't paint that. It's good wood."

> Riskless is hardly worth your effort.
> — SETH GODIN

Your mother-in-law stops by (I pick on mothers-in-law because I have a really good one who doesn't say things like this, so she won't mind), and she, in all of her well-meaning glory, says, "You can't just paint that. You have to strip it and sand it. You should have a professional do that. You'll ruin it."

So you look at your eight-dollar yard-sale table that's been sitting in the garage for six months, and you are suddenly afraid that you will ruin it. The thought of sanding and stripping and other words you can't remember is too overwhelming, so what do you do? You let it sit another six months, and then you either sell it at your next yard sale for five dollars or you drop it off at Goodwill.

Then a local blogger buys it, doesn't strip it, doesn't prime it, just slaps some leftover paint on it, and it turns out great — not perfect, not award winning, but it looks lovely in her home and holds a coffee cup and a stack of books. When you see it on her blog, it looks eerily familiar. No, it won't be sold by Sotheby's, but unless it

RIGHT Dried out stumps from the yard, used as tables

was that rare hidden gem, it didn't have a chance anyway.

The moral of the story: you can't ruin something that you don't like, especially if it doesn't have much value to begin with.

I wouldn't tell you to take your first risk with a hand-me-down antique. But an eight-dollar yard-sale table that sat in your garage for six months? What do you have to lose? You are out eight dollars if it turns out bad. You can drop it off at the dump under the cover of night if it turns out disgraceful. But if it would have turned out great and you never risked it, you've lost a great addition to your home.

The Art of Risk

We don't risk because it's easy; we risk because of hope, because we see the promise of something better.

If you insist on worrying about things, worry about a meteor hitting the earth. Worry about your car's brakes failing or your teeth and hair falling out within a month of each other. Stop worrying about decorating. It's supposed to be fun.

The key to creating a beautiful home isn't knowing what you are doing; it's taking a risk even if you *don't* know what you are doing. There *is* no wrong way to create beauty.

So go do something now and hope that it's less than perfect so you can figure out right away that less than perfect won't kill you, unless you are measuring out lye to make soap or creating the atom bomb.

Go forth and take a risk.

CHAPTER 7

Well-Intentioned Voices

the order to be irreplaceable, one must always be different.

– Coco Chanel

"IN ORDER to be irreplaceable one must always be different."
—Coco Chanel

When all think alike,
then no one is thinking.

— WALTER LIPPMAN

For Women with Opinionated People in Their Lives

I got an email from Sabrina awhile back. She couldn't figure out why nothing looked right on her fireplace and mantel. After I looked at the photos, it was clear to me that she didn't need new accessories. She needed painted brick. She had a huge wall of dated, multihued brick that sucked up all the light in the room. When I broke the news to her, she took it swell. Then she informed me that she simply couldn't paint the brick because her uncle is a bricklayer, and he had already voiced his opinion that it was dumb to paint over perfectly good brick. End of story. She couldn't possibly paint her brick, because her uncle thought that was a poor choice.

How many times have we let our uncles, our dads, our mothers-in-law, or our painters make decorating decisions for us?

Sabrina and I chatted some more, and I think she has decided to paint after all. I suggested that as long as she's not planning to ask her uncle to paint the brick himself or have him pay for the paint or the mortgage on the house, then she shouldn't feel compelled to take decorating advice from him. (Husbands are a different story because they usually *are* paying the mortgage or the rent, but they get a whole section of their own.)

Spouses, sisters, dads, fathers-in-law, interior-designer friends, and neighbors can wreak havoc on a fragile little design plan. How do you know when to smile and move on, and when to change your plans?

Here are questions I frequently get asked at Nesting Place:

- "How do I get my husband to agree to hang a chandelier over our bed?"
- "My painter told me not to paint the trim and walls white but to go with off-white for the walls, and now I hate it! Help!"
- "My mother-in-law says my house is so white inside it looks like a hospital, but I think it looks clean and fresh! What do I do?"

When you are already questioning your choices, it's hard to know what to do with advice, whether it's solicited or not.

Here's how I decide how much weight to assign a person's opinion.

Think about that one thing that you are kind of an expert in. Maybe it's shopping organic or dressing great on a budget or being the boss at your corporate job. Whatever that thing is, you are good at it, and you know it. It's not a cocky kind of knowing but a quiet confidence that you have enough experience to make smart decisions.

> But what happens when people offer suggestions about an area in which we're not confident?

So when a well-meaning friend tries to tell you how to do that thing, you are kind enough to smile and nod, but you know you'll never do it that way because you have enough experience to make a good decision without her help. Say your mom says you should shop at Walmart because it's cheaper and has great clothes. That's nice. But you know that you like Target better. Walmart is great for her; Target is great for you. You don't worry that you need to start shopping someplace else just to please her, because you are confident in your choice. You are polite and then buy yourself some cute Mossimo jeans.

But what happens when people offer suggestions about an area in which we're not confident? What if that area is creating a home and decorating? We get confused, we worry we'll hurt their feelings, and we find ourselves paralyzed. Once again, perfectionism rises to the surface and we wonder whether they know us better than we know ourselves, so we spend all our time listening to the opinions of others instead of figuring out what *we* like.

Your painter with the coveralls, mustache, and pickup truck is an expert at putting paint on walls (hopefully). He may or may not be an expert at picking out what paint colors you will like. Every single painter I have ever hired (which is only two, but still) tried to get me to change my mind on something and told me I was doing it wrong. I thanked him and repeated over and over to myself that if he were an expert at picking great colors, he'd be a designer. One painter refused even to give me a quote on painting our exterior brick, claiming I'd ruin our house and nobody paints brick. Fine with me. I just hired the next guy.

But often we listen to bad advice out of fear (we're afraid we'll make a mistake) and sometimes out of laziness (we don't want to put the work into getting familiar with making well-informed decisions).

When we lived in Our Imperfect Average Dream House, I chose our exterior paint color after spending a good month driving around town taking pictures of houses with paint colors I liked. And this was before the advent of the inconspicuous camera phone. I narrowed it down to two houses and knocked on the owners' doors to ask about the paint color. (Yes, you can do that! They'll take it as a huge compliment.) Both colors were the same, so I knew my color.

Driving around town with a camera was a pain, and I felt like a creepy stalker or a secret service agent. Did I mention I had three young boys in my SUV while doing this? It wasn't easy. But it was the work I needed to do so I could make a wise choice.

The best place to start with making your own decorating decisions is to

practice taking little risks until it gets easier. It won't be long before you can face the painter and tell him you are picking your own paint colors, thank you very much. *You* get to create beauty in your own home for you and your family.

So how do you know whose opinion to listen to when it comes to well-meaning friends and family members?

I never take decorating advice from someone whose house I don't like. If I can't appreciate her style or find real beauty there, there's no reason to consider her opinion. (In fact, if you really dislike someone's taste, you could make a mental note to consider the opposite of what they suggest. How fun!)

> The best place to start with making your own decorating decisions is to practice taking little risks until it gets easier.

Often at Nesting Place, people give me advice, telling me to paint my wall or move the sofa. I admit I click over to their website. If I like what I see, I'll consider their opinion. If it's totally not my style and I don't like their wall color or where they put *their* sofa, I'll ignore the suggestion. Many times they don't have a website or a blog that has photos of their house, and you know what I do with their suggestion? Put it out of my mind, because I really don't know where it's coming from.

I do listen to people who have created the kind of home that I want to have. I don't care if they are not designers, if they don't have degrees, or if they don't think they know what they are doing. If I have a friend whose home I love, I'll ask her advice when I'm making a decorating decision.

Get advice from people who are doing the thing the way you want to be doing that thing. It's a universal law that can be applied to almost any situation.

On Husbands

I'm often asked at Nesting Place questions about husbands and decorating, so I thought husbands deserved their very own section. If you don't have a husband, feel free to skip ahead to the next chapter. If you are a husband, feel free to email me and tell me I'm wrong about what I say here.

I want my husband to love our home. It's his place too. So of course I want him to enjoy it, feel at home, and feel that it represents who he is. I value his opinion, and I've also learned where to draw the line. That's the nice way of saying that if I ask him whether I should get 200-thread-count sheets or 1,000-thread-count sheets, he'll probably feel compelled to come up with some sort of answer, but most likely he doesn't really care. Over time I've gained his trust enough that he wants me to make that kind of decision. It's a win-win. (And who wouldn't want 1,000-thread-count sheets?)

I've found, though, that often we ask our husbands for advice when we are unsure of what to do. Then we blame them if we don't like the color of the new bathroom rug, when they didn't really care what color it was in the first place. They were just answering a question that we asked out of obligation or lack of confidence. It helps to figure out what things your husband cares about and get his input on those things, and then don't bother him with the rest.

Consider this interaction with a Nesting Place reader, Alana:

 Hello, Nester! I was hoping to gain your insight on something, since I know you're all about creating an intentional home. I have developed a love for decorating over the past several years, to the point that I'd love to do it for other people, at least on a consulting basis. Up until now, my husband and I have had zero wiggle room in the budget, much less extra funds to decorate. But now we have a tiny bit that I could use, and I'm totally ready to thrift and DIY my way to what I want. But my problem isn't money . . . It's my honey! (See what I did there . . .) My hubby and I have polar opposite styles. Everything I like, he doesn't, and vice versa. My goal was to involve him and create a space we both love, but it's just not working. I haven't done one. Single. Thing. Because we just cannot agree. So my question is: Do you allow your husband to "have a say"? Or are you just blessed to have one of those guys who shares your taste or truly doesn't have an opinion on "girly stuff" like curtains and paint colors? Thanks for your help!

Alana

 Hey Alana, well, I think I'm one of those girls whose husband doesn't care to be in on every design detail. And also we have some of the same taste. If I wanted to do all pink walls, I'm sure he'd question it. But over time, I've earned his trust. At first, he questioned small things, but then he'd like the end result. So the next time, he completely let me make the decision. Now, he 100%-ish lets me do what I want, although I always try to get his opinion on big things. So I'd start with something small and "prove" you know what you are doing. Make a pinboard on Pinterest and show him where you are going. Also, sometimes my husband will give me his honest opinion because I asked, but when it comes down to it, he really doesn't care which pillows I pick. So don't ask unless his opinion really matters.

Myquillyn

Makes perfect sense. I keep asking my hubby about every last detail, and he gives his opinion. But I think I'll try your suggestion going forward: take liberty with the small things and earn his trust, then consult him on the bigger things that can't be changed so easily or are expensive. Thanks for the insight. I had to email because I had reached such a point of frustration. It was hard to have such a love for decor but no way to express it.

Alana

Here's another scenario. Let's say you've been perusing Pinterest, and you are convinced that your guest room needs a beautiful black wall. Your husband gets home from a long day at work, and you are so excited about the possibility of the life-changing black wall that the first thing you ask him is if he can paint the guest-room wall black this weekend.

You have a 98 percent chance of getting a no.

Here are the problems: First, your timing is all wrong. Don't ask him to do something right when he gets home from doing something. No one responds well to that.

Second, he will most likely see no need for a black wall. Men are logical, and there's no reason to go to the trouble of fixing something that ain't broke.

Third, he may not believe a black wall is a good choice. Translation: he doesn't fully trust your judgment.

The good news is you can have a big impact on each of these objections if you have a little patience.

The first issue is the easiest to fix. I try not to bring up new things when my husband isn't in the right mood to hear them. Wait until after dinner.

Also, I find that when I bring up something in the context of how excited I am and how happy it would make me to try it, he's usually up for it. He's smart and he's learned that the whole family benefits when something makes me happy. And that's a little secret: you know how he knows that something has made me happy? Because when something makes me happy, I tell him. Then — get this — I *be* happy.

So that means your next project starts with your last project. Follow me here. If his reward for having a black wall is a happy wife, then he should know that you'll be happy because happiness was your reaction to the last little project you did. However, if the last project was full of angst, tears, and his doing a lot of work and your doing a lot of complaining, you can pretty much guarantee your chances of doing another project anytime soon are scant. So let your husband know that you think a project is worth it and that it brings you joy. Especially if you're asking him to do some of the work!

If you are already in the hole because your last home project caused fights and wailing and gnashing of teeth, you'll have some work to do before you introduce

The good news is you can have a big impact on each of these objections if you have a little patience.

A CHEAP, lightweight grandfather clock that I painted white. I removed the clock face, painted it with chalkboard paint, and painted the word whenever over and over again.

OUR BOYS LEARNED to paint walls in this, our bonus room. We started them off with an easy room using the same color for the walls, ceiling, and trim.

another project. My suggestion is to find little projects you can do on your own without his help. Create little wins with small risks and move up from there. Spray-paint a frame or make a wreath or buy some pillows. And if you hate it and it all falls apart, *do not, under any circumstances*, go crying or complaining to your husband in this part of the process. If your husband is the person whom you complain to about your house-decorating pursuits, he will want to find a way to help make you not cry or complain in the future, because he loves you and doesn't want you to be sad and frustrated. His reasoning will be that the easiest way to make sure you don't cry is to make sure you don't do any more house projects. You are shooting yourself in the foot. Ouch.

So wait until you've completed a little project that you are happy with and then show it to him and tell him how happy that makes you. And don't forget this last important step: after you tell him how happy it makes you, be happy! Over time he'll see that fixing up the house brings you joy, and he'll be more open to doing such things in the future.

The second issue in the black-wall scenario is that he simply sees no need for it and so doesn't want to put the time and effort into helping. We need to be thoughtful and not ask other people to do a bunch of work that we are perfectly capable of doing. This is how I look at it: in any given year, my husband will agree to do a certain amount of house fixing-upping. I want to use that time wisely, so I'm not going to use up his skills on things that I can do. I can paint a wall. You can paint a wall. We can paint walls.

Maybe you have the type of husband who doesn't want you to have to paint a wall. You get to decide how to handle that. But wall painting is easier and less risky than learning to drive a car. Unless the room has tall ceilings or some special circumstance, this is a great opportunity for you to learn a new skill. Or consider hiring it out. Either way, I've found it's best to save my requests for things only he can do.

Last, maybe he thinks a black wall is the worst idea in the history of ever. If someone thinks something is a bad idea logically, they use information they already know about you to decide whether your bad idea is worth pursuing. So remind him of the last time he thought something you did was a bad idea and it turned out great. If you don't have a time like that or if you have a history of bad ideas, you might first want to create some bad ideas gone right with something small — again, little wins.

Ultimately, you want your husband, your family, and yourself to enjoy the home you are creating, even while you are creating it. If the reward for your work in the house is a complaining, bossy, ill-content wife/mom/self, don't be surprised if your husband puts a moratorium on future decorating projects. You might even want to thank him for it. On the other hand, if you are able to approach beautifying and cozifying your home with a fun, lighthearted attitude, your rooms and your family will benefit.

On Painting Walls

If you've never painted a wall before, you should practice first. You could practice in the closet or in the garage or help your friend who has painted before paint her walls. What's the worst that can happen? (I'll tell you, the worst is that you spill the entire can of paint. Which I have done. On laminate floor. In a rental. And I lived to tell about it.)

There are sixteen million how-to-paint-a-wall YouTube videos available. Watch some. Then buy a gallon of paint. The paint dude at the local home improvement store can help you decide on a finish or sheen for the paint, depending on the room.

If you paint a wall and hate the color, that's not a big deal. I promise. Once you get your groove on, it takes thirty dollars and about two and a half hours to paint a room. In the scope of life, that's not that risky. You can always paint over it in a few weeks or, if you are especially spunky, the next day.

Also, don't ever choose a paint color in the paint store. It will look different in your house (unless you live in a home improvement store with thirty-foot ceilings and fluorescent lights). It's a great idea to buy the smallest sample amount of the paint you are considering. Then find the largest piece of poster board you can and paint it with your sample color. Tack up the poster board in different parts of the room to see whether you like it. Tuck it next to the window behind the drapes, in the center of the wall behind the mirror. Live with it and see how the color changes with the sunlight.

CHAPTER 8

Lovely Limitations

THIS COZY AREA was completed on a budget with a twenty-dollar thrifted chair, free stumps for tables, book page wreath I made myself from less than ten dollars' worth of supplies, eighty dollar Ikea Expedit Shelf, and a sixteen-dollar pillow from HomeGoods. The splurge was the room-sized, 8-by-10 herringbone cowhide run that I purchased online at a flash sale site for $600 dollars.

Much of the beauty that arises in art comes from the struggle an artist wages with his limited medium.

— HENRI MATISSE

When Buts Get in the Way

Let's talk about buts.

We all love to point out our buts. We all believe our buts are special, and no one else has a but like ours. Our buts hold us back. Our buts have become a wonderful excuse to put off, whine, and give up. And just like the kind of butts with skin on them, we sometimes assume that if we just had a different but, our lives would be easier. Instead of learning to appreciate and use our buts to get us where we are going, we see them as holding us back.

In our home, our buts can look many different ways.

- I'd love to move our sofa, *but* it's always been under the window.
- *You* can create a beautiful family room, *but* I can't because we homeschool.
- I long to have a bedroom that's relaxing and peaceful, *but* I don't have the money.

I love that Henri Matisse quote up there at the beginning of the chapter, and it's even more meaningful when it's adapted to talk specifically about our houses. I don't think Henri would mind: much of the beauty that arises in our homes comes from the struggle we wage with our limited resources.

Our buts are our limited resources. Our buts are the catalyst to creativity. If it weren't for our buts, our homes wouldn't be as beautiful.

Let's flesh out (hate me, I couldn't resist) the common types of buts we run into when it comes to decorating.

But I Don't Have the Money

The number one obstacle for women who want to make changes in their homes is the assumption that they need an enormous amount of money. The truth is it does take some money, but you get to decide how much.

No matter what you do to get furniture, paint, and items for your home, there's a cost — time, money, and energy. You get to decide which resource you have the most of at any given time. If you don't have a lot of money to spend, then you can make up for that with time or energy. For example, if you don't have the money to hire a painter to paint your dining room, you can spend more of your time to get creative and find someone to barter with to get your space painted, or you can spend your energy and just paint it yourself. It takes more than money to make a room beautiful; if you have abundant time and/or energy, you can make a huge difference in your spaces. We'll talk super specific in chapter 10 about how to save money while beautificating.

Never having much money for decorating is the *very first* thing that forced me to get creative in our home. It's made me smart, inventive, and attentive, and I'm not just saying that because it sounds nice in a book like this. It's true, and eighteen years ago, I would have been the last person to believe it. All of the best things I've done in our house are a result of having to think differently and come up with an inexpensive solution.

I've started calling dreadful circumstances Lovely Limitations.

Lovely Limitations come in many forms. A tiny budget is a Lovely Limitation, but so is a tiny room without any windows. A room with an awkward corner fireplace could be a Lovely Limitation. Renting a place with ugly carpet, having to incorporate your husband's favorite chair into the design scheme, and having no overhead lighting could all be seen as Lovely Limitations.

Lovely Limitations aren't bad. They are springboards to the creative solutions that often make a room far better than it would have been without that final push. It's like what your grandmother always said about problems being blessings in disguise. We may think it would be easier to work without the limitations of an odd-shaped room or a tight budget or two preschoolers carrying sippy cups, but having no limits can be debilitating. When you have no limits, you put off making a decision because there are so many options. I've gotten to the point of craving limits, because I know that some of my best projects have come out of what I *didn't* have.

THIS RAMSHACKLE, hate-at-first-sight renters fireplace has been featured in *Better Homes and Gardens' Do It Yourself Magazine*, *Better Homes and Gardens' Christmas Ideas* magazine, and *Cottages and Bungalows* — all because I hated it so much that I had to change it within my limitations. The black part with white bricks is chalkboard contact paper with drawn-on bricks.

Top Eleven Reasons Renting Is Awesome

1. You get to decide every year (or however often your lease is) whether you want to move. Don't underestimate this. Freedom like this has great value. To me this is the biggest perk of renting.

2. When they rezone your area and decide to build a garbage dump or sewage treatment place or nuclear waste plant or some other horrible thing that homeowners have nightmares about, you just don't renew your lease.

3. The more houses you live in, the more you learn your likes and dislikes. Renting a few different houses in a short time is a great way to gather up a lot of research about yourself and use that information during your future house purchase. Think of it as house research, no lab coat required.

4. All those big issues — mold, roofs, plumbing, electrical, termites? You don't even have to worry about paying for those. Every time something breaks, it's a reminder to be happy that you don't have to fix it.

5. If some bacon grease accidentally goes down the drain, you don't care. (Not that that's ever happened to me.)

6. In our town, we can rent a better house than we could buy with the same amount of money per month. So as we save up for our next purchase, we can live it up in a neighborhood with a pool.

7. Renter's insurance is much less expensive than homeowner's insurance.

8. Living in a house that isn't your style or isn't your first choice (or even tenth choice) of where to live can give you great perspective: this world is not your home.

9. If something unforeseeable happens and your income is no longer what it was, you don't have to worry about defaulting on your mortgage. You just talk to your landlord, work something out, and if need be look for a less expensive place to live.

10. When the housing market plummets, you are secretly happy because that means you might get to buy a house. Or at least there will be lots more rentals available, which means you might find cheaper rent for a better place.

11. Renting is one of the Loveliest Limitations you'll ever experience. Nothing forces you to be more creative than working around someone else's decorating choices, choices you might not be able to change. Some of my most-loved creative endeavors in our home are the result of being limited with my choices because we were renters. What a gift!

The thing is if you spend all your time fretting over the fact that you live in your parents' basement or in an ugly rental or a house with no windows, you won't have any energy left to create a home right where you are. So don't cheat on your current house by dreaming of the life you'll have with your next house.

Embrace the limitation, recognize it for what it is, and consider it a dare to overcome it. Decide to accept the resources that you have been trusted with, however small or great they are. Choose to see the possibilities. You have what it takes to try. Creating a beautiful home is an art that develops with time. The sooner you start and the more risks you are willing to take, the more quickly you learn how to create something you love.

But I Can't Change That

One of the first things I noticed about our current Home Because It's Where We Are rental was the fireplace surround: it was yellow. I don't mean a soft, how-cheery-and-charming yellow, but yellow-teeth yellow. I wanted to change our fireplace, but we were renting. I just showed you my but. Did you miss it? What could I possibly do that was temporary but clever enough to look better and hold up to a fire burning in the fireplace? Forget it!

I spent a few weeks (okay, months — it was months before I came up with the solution) with the surround at the forefront of my brain. I don't mean that I thought about it all the time, but my mind was always paying attention to anything that could be a solution.

Then one day I came across vinyl stick-on sheets of chalkboard paper. Just like the old contact paper we used to use to cover our textbooks, only thicker with chalkboardish material on the front. I ordered some, cut it up, and tried it out. I knew it could be a huge waste, but the outcome, if good, outweighed the risk. I didn't need to announce to the world I was using chalkboard contact paper on our fireplace surround — unless it worked.

And it did! Attention, world, come look at this fun solution that I never would have looked for had it not been a problem in the first place. Our firebox is large

GALLERY WALL, a renter's best friend for instant personality

enough and our gas fireplace is gentle enough that the chalkboard surround has lasted for years. And I can easily remove it at any time.

One more thing: sure, I could have left my chalkboard material plain, but it was a *chalkboard* after all. So I drew imperfect bricks on it with white chalk markers.

Suddenly, the one thing in our family room that I hated the most became the very thing I wanted to show off.

I know what you're thinking: *Wait, you can't DO that. You can't put chalkboard vinyl stick-on sheets around your fireplace!* I thought that too at first. But I decided to ignore that voice, and I'm glad I did. Shock of all shocks, shelter magazines liked the chalkboard fireplace too. It's been photographed and published three times. The fireplace I hated has become a showpiece, but more important, it's one of my favorite things in the room. I'm so glad I had a less-than-acceptable-to-me fireplace — a *but* if you will — otherwise I never would have cared to change it up.

> The best rooms are usually the result of good old-fashioned trial and error.

I find that people are interested in the creative process of creating a beautiful room, but often they don't like what they hear. We are looking for a magic formula, a step-by-step, foolproof way to decorate, and it just doesn't exist. The best rooms are usually the result of good old-fashioned trial and error, risk, meaningful beauty, a bunch of unwanted Lovely Limitations, random buts we have to overcome, and some tears thrown in for good measure.

Let that be an encouragement to you, because all of those ingredients are readily available to all of us, whether we want them or not.

Too Many Options But

For a few years, our bedroom sat untouched except for a coat of gray paint on the walls. I had Pinterest boards and stacks of magazines and even a few swatches of fabric all at the ready; there were *so* many great ideas I had for this room. But I didn't know where to start. So there it sat, frozen in time.

Finally, last year a duct-tape company challenged some DIY bloggers to do a project with duct tape. All they required was that we use the tape in our homes; there were no parameters. But I have a sickness: I want to be recognized as extremely creative and surprise people with my talents. It's a pride thing; I get it. I also don't like to spend a huge amount of time without making a huge impact. That's a nice way to say I'm selectively lazy. But I prefer to say I'm smart with my time. So my challenge was to use the tape in a creative way that had a big impact in relation to the time spent.

THIS UNORTHODOX USE of white duct tape on the wall got the attention of the *Baltimore Sun* and *Better Homes and Gardens' Christmas Ideas* magazine.

But you used tape on your walls? That white stuff? It's the actual tape? Not paint? Yes! My husband and I took an afternoon and measured and marked off the spaces where the strips of tape would meet. And then we simply taped lines over the marks in one direction, then the other. We had no idea whether it would work or whether, if it did, we would like the results, but it was worth the risk. The decorating police haven't put me in their trendy jail complete with lined window treatments, no one has laughed at me (at least not to my face), and I expect our walls to need a light sanding and a good thick coat of paint when we remove the tape. Totally worth it.

This room was finished as a result of a challenge to simply "use duct tape." I'm so glad I had a limitation, otherwise I never would have finished the room and I wouldn't love it as much as I do. I'd still be scrolling through a long Pinterest board full of too many beautiful options.

You know how you get so much done right before company comes? You have no choice. Sometimes it's helpful to set some limits on ourselves just to jump-start our creativity. If you need that push to get you started so you can finish the guest room, invite an overnight guest next month. I promise your guest room will look better in a few weeks.

When everything is an option, it's overwhelming. Embracing and choosing to work with a limit for a space is the first step to creating a beautiful room. The question is where to start.

CHAPTER 9

One Room
at a Time

The beginning is always today.

— MARY SHELLEY

How to Start

Creating a beautiful home starts in your head, not in the furniture store.

With any project, you don't begin by focusing on what you need; you begin with recognizing what you already have. I wasted years in our early homes fretting over what I *didn't* have, and it blinded me to what was right in front of me.

Most of us already have three vital things when it comes to creating the home we've always longed for:

1. EVERY HOUSE HAS A REDEEMING QUALITY. Wherever you live right now, there is something in your home that works well for you, some function or form that serves your family, something you find beautiful. Maybe it's the layout with an open kitchen or a screened-in porch that doubles as a playroom in the summer. Maybe you love the old leaded glass windows. Sometimes that redeeming quality is the result of a Lovely Limitation. The best way to start creating a beautiful home is by being grateful for what you already have.

The family room in our current home is long and narrow, and when we first moved in, I wondered how I could possibly fill the awkward space in front of the double window next to the corner fireplace. At the same time, I had three boys who were doing all of their schoolwork at the kitchen table. Our poor kitchen table was a workhorse. Projects, homework, laundry — there was barely room for eating.

Then I remembered I had an old forty-dollar Kmart table in the garage that wasn't being used to its fullest potential. I gave it a fresh coat of paint and set it in front of

My office consists of a seventy-five-dollar yard-sale armoire (a Spanish wood Rooms to Go piece that everyone in America has had at some point, painted with Behr paint plus primer); an eighty-five-dollar dresser that I took a door off of, put baskets in, and painted the same as the armoire; a fifteen-dollar yard-sale kitchen table; and an upholstered chair I've had for years. None of it came from an office-supply store, and each piece can be used in a different way in a different room if the need arises.

the windows with a few upholstered chairs. Suddenly everyone was fighting to sit at the "homework table" to do their homework in the family room. Yep, we had a kitchen table a mere ten feet from another kitchen table, but it worked well for us, and I made it my mission to make it beautiful. And you know what people said when they came over? "I wish I had room for a table in my family room." The very thing that I looked at as a problem became an opportunity to do something unique that served our family well.

I bet your home has something like that, whether you are in an apartment, an empty, intimidating dream house, your in-laws' basement, a rental, or a home fully decorated in a style that's not your own. Maybe there is a nook that could be cozy with a small chair and a lamp, or charming sloped ceilings, or a long hallway begging to become a gallery wall full of family photos. Instead of looking at the things you hate about where you are, start to look for the positives, either the areas you've used well or the missed opportunities. Every home has a silver lining.

2. EVERYONE HAS PIECES. Yes, I know your bed is old and your sofa is falling apart or you have beautiful things but they are just not your style. But surely there's something you love. Even if you are really unhappy with the state of your home, I'm guessing it's not empty. You have things in your home, and some of those things have a lot of decorating flexibility. Instead of starting out furnishing a room with a drive to the furniture store, take stock of the potential of what you already have. The small dresser from the closet or the wooden chair in the attic might look great with a new coat of paint.

If you are like me, you have a limited amount of funds, so buying all new items at one time is out of the question. I've learned the art of using things I have in different ways. You don't have to announce to the world that you are using a pair of small wingback chairs at the ends of your dining room table; just put them there and see if you like them.

Recently I changed out a smaller oval mirror for a large rectangle. And I was in the mood for change, so I mixed up some paint and quickly painted it the perfect shade of coral. The perfect shade of coral when it was in the mixing pot, that is. Once I painted the mirror, it was too strawberry. So I added more paint — too orange. More paint — too barbie. More paint — too much the color of throw-up. Currently I have a throw-up-colored mirror in my office. Not the look I'm going for, but still better than it was before. I'll change it up again when the mood hits in the next few weeks.

3. EVERYONE HAS MEANINGFUL BEAUTY.

This is one of the most important parts of any space. It's what separates a house from a home — the meaningful, personal mementos. Meaningful beauty can be:

- Books
- Kids' rock collection
- Grandma's chipped blue-and-white china
- Husband's guitar and Grandpa's fiddle with the broken strings
- That box of old letters
- Toys! What? Yes, display the Lego creations or add some plastic dinosaurs to your terrarium or plants.
- Collected shells
- Framed pieces of flatware
- Photos

Meaningful beauty is the best kind of beauty around. A pretty vase is nice. But a pretty vase handed down from your great-aunt is even better.

Most of us have meaningful beauty packed away safely in our closets and attics. Consider the beautiful, meaningful pieces that you already have and how they can be worked into a finished room.

Where Do I Begin?

I find it's easier and less stressful for the family, the dog, and myself if I focus on one room at a time when I'm redecorating. I like to start with the room we spend the most time in as a family. There's no wrong place to start. Some designers say to start with the master bedroom — how could that be wrong? You will never regret that. But for me, I've always started in the family room. The room where my family spends most of our in-house time awake and together. Then, roughly, I move through the following steps.

> It doesn't matter if my neighbor uses the same room in their house for something different. I get to decide what would work best for our family right now.

Determine the Purpose of the Room

The first thing I do is consider the main purpose of the room and any secondary purposes. It doesn't matter if my neighbor uses the same room in their house for something different. I get to decide what would work best for our family right now. How do we need this room to serve us?

Let's take the family room for example. The main purpose of our family room in this season of our life is for hanging out with friends and family. However, hanging out happens in different ways at different times: watching the big game and movies, sitting around the fire, playing board games, eating pizza, tripping over the dog, drinking and spilling drinks that stain. But also your children use it to do homework and you like to read in the family room and you and your husband like to sit in the chairs with your laptops.

Given these purposes, you know you need to have comfy seating for watching TV and also viewing the fireplace (or seating that can be easily moved to the fireplace or TV), a surface for playing games, a surface that works well for spread-out homework, lamps for reading, and at least one comfy chair near an outlet, and everything needs to be made of materials that won't have to be thrown away when pizza sauce gets smeared all over (sorry, no silk sofa for this room).

Now you know what direction you want to go, but how do you get there?

Find Your Muse

After you've determined the primary and secondary purposes of the room, I suggest finding a muse. Start a Pinterest board, rip out pages of magazines, and find other ways to get some images in your head of the feel you are going for. This isn't so you can copy but so you have a guide to help keep you on track.

OUR FAMILY ROOM has evolved over the years. White slipcovers and walls have turned out to be a great canvas for a room full of meaningful beauty.

What Kind of Thinker Are You?

Sometimes change in our homes has to start with a change in our thinking. There are two main types of people who are unhappy with their homes:

The Overthinkers

You don't love your home, and you are out and see a pretty trinket that you are drawn to. It's not expensive, it makes you happy, and for whatever reason it brings a little meaning to you. You think it's just your style. But you don't buy it because you have no idea what you will do with it. You go home to your empty house and wonder why it's so cold and uninviting. You have empty rooms and empty tables, and your husband keeps encouraging you to get a few things to make your house feel like a home. You should go back out and purchase that little trinket. But you are afraid of making the wrong choice, so you do nothing. You think you're safe because you aren't taking any chances, but the cost of your risklessness is a non-homey home.

The Underthinkers

You don't love your home, and you are out and see a pretty trinket that you are drawn to. It's not expensive, it makes you happy, and for whatever reason it brings a little meaning to you. You think it's just your style. So you buy it. And you come home and cram it onto the coffee table with all of your other meaningful trinkets. Your husband asks how much you spent, and you tell him it was just a few dollars, so neither of you sees a problem. But really you should take it back because you have enough trinkets. You are putting all of your time and energy into little trinkets when your walls need to be painted, or maybe your home is actually finished in a way and you are avoiding the next thing you are meant to be doing. You think it's not a big deal because it was just a few dollars and you can sell it at your next yard sale. In five years, you realize you have a part-time job purchasing trinkets and then selling them for a fraction of the price at yard sales that you don't feel like having.

For years I was an Underthinker. I still struggle with it. But it helps me just to know what my tendencies are. What kind of thinker are you? Being aware of your fears and temptations may not change everything about how you decorate, but it will help you get started and still finish well.

Quieting a room is one of my favorite things to do.

After our summer visits to The Cottage, I came home with a fresh perspective and wondered if there were some renter-friendly changes I could make that would help me love our home's canvas, its bones, even if it were empty.

Over the years, I had overcompensated for the lack of character in our rental home with a bunch of crowded cute accessories. We didn't have a pretty fireplace, so I tried to hide it by overfilling the mantel with the latest accessories. Instead of looking like a pretty fireplace, it looked like a cluttered fireplace.

Before I added anything more, I needed to prep my canvas.

Quiet the Room

So I quieted the space. Sometimes a room is so full of the everyday things we've been looking at for years that we can't even see what we've got. We can't see the forest for the trees. Or we can't see the sofa for the cute pillows.

Quieting a room is one of my favorite things to do. I try to do it in each room at least once a year, but I was especially eager to do so after I left The Cottage. If you are an Overthinker, you may not have as much to remove from any given room, but it's still a good exercise.

First, find a holding area near the room but out of the way enough that you can leave a stack of stuff there for a day

or so without driving everyone in your house insane or scaring the dog.

Next, remove everything that isn't a rug, piece of furniture, lamp, or somehow attached to the wall (drapes and wall art can stay). Take out all the little junk on your tables, mantel, and ottomans; the baskets of magazines; the picture frames; the papers; the bills; the clay bowls your daughter made. Remove the throw pillows and the blankets and the stack of puzzles and books. Take out the plants and candles and toys and everything else.

Now you should have a quieter room, a room with just artwork and furniture and drapes and a lamp or two or, if you are me, four.

The first time I quieted the house after staying at The Cottage, I realized just how much I was depending on tchotchkes and little personality-filled accessories to set the tone for our home. Once I forced myself to remove all the little decorative items I had collected in our family room, I realized I didn't like what I saw: walls that needed a fresh coat of paint, dated busy drapes, and a large daunting expanse of wall I couldn't seem to get right. We had lived in our rental home for two years, and I was trying to compensate for furniture that was no longer my style and walls I didn't feel like painting by purchasing an ever-rotating parade of ten-dollar tchotchkes, hoping the next cute little bauble would help me like my room better.

What I really wanted was a different-colored wood floor, a hefty mantel, and a stone fireplace. If we owned this house, those are things I could have considered over time. Put bluntly, I didn't believe our average, no-frills rental home had beautiful bones. How was I going to create my nice blank canvas? But I could see that I could change a lot with a different pattern on my chairs, fresh window treatments, paint on the walls, and a gallery wall full of meaningful artwork. Of course, we were renting, so I had to be extra creative, and I couldn't buy all new furniture. I needed to find inexpensive, easy, renter-friendly ways to turn our family room into a room I loved.

Enter My Lovely Limitations

Quieting the space also helps us see things that we love that have been hidden under

stacks of magazines and afghans. Without all the stuff in a room, we can see the room itself and decide what can stay (maybe with a little update), what needs to finally retire, and whether there's something the room desperately needs that we've been avoiding. For example, after I quieted our family room, I realized that I was tired of the pattern of the sofa's upholstery. But the sofa had outstanding scale and comfort, and I realized I didn't need to replace it; I just needed to update it. A few months later, I gathered some friends and we had a slipcover-making party. Twelve hours later, I had a fresh white slipcover for our sofa.

Once you quiet the space, leave the room like that for at least a day and see how it feels. I'm always surprised at how much my family is starved for cleared-off surfaces. Once when I quieted the family room, my boys brought down their Legos to play on the freshly cleared coffee table. That's when I stopped trying to "style" the coffee table in the family room. I no longer fill it up with decorative items to the

A QUIET ROOM after our second trip to the cottage, and a slipcovered sofa. It's moving right along.

point where there's no room for what we need to use. Everyday living became more important than staging our coffee table. Besides, if I could create a room where I loved the canvas, or the bones, then not having a styled coffee table probably wouldn't even be that noticeable.

Prep Your Canvas

Once you see what you have after quieting the house, you'll probably find some gaps you need to fill to make the space work harder for your family. Time to change some things up. And if you are making changes anyway, why not pursue both form and function? Look for items that work for your family that also are beautiful.

Over the years, after quieting the family room, I've made a mental list of changes I wanted to make, things like eye-catching window treatments, a slipcover for the sofa, large-scale meaningful art, additional comfy seating, and fresh paint in a shade of white that played down the pinkness of the floors.

> Suddenly the most inexpensive basic windows in the world became a pretty focal point.

One year, I decided to take advantage of the plethora of windows on the back of our house in the breakfast area that adjoins the family room. I removed all the blinds, labeled them, and stored them in the attic. Then I painted the room a fresh shade of white with just enough green in it to neutralize the pink in our floors. (I took a chance and decided I was doing the owners a favor by painting over the thin coat of flat builder-grade paint.)

Suddenly the most inexpensive basic windows in the world became a pretty focal point. I decided not to put anything on them because they looked so pretty naked. Lucky windows. The blind-free, window-filled room turned out to be a nice blank canvas. After a couple of coats of paint on our dining table and hutch, a new large-scale light fixture, and inexpensive Ikea chairs, I had a room I loved.

All of these changes came about because of two things: (1) I found a muse that motivated and inspired me, and (2) I quieted the house and evaluated what I had and what I needed.

The family room took a little more work and time. I needed some extra seating, a few more surfaces, and larger artwork. But I didn't run out to the furniture store. That's not much fun, and it's not always the best place to spend my budget. Instead I gave myself lots of time to create a room that represented and served our family, despite our Lovely Limitations. I also gave myself permission to take risks and ruin thirty-dollar pieces of furniture.

I found lots of ways to furnish our home without spending a bunch of cash. We're going to look at those methods and tricks in the next chapter.

TIP: when using white, use eggshell finish and paint the trim and walls all out of the same can of paint.

CHAPTER 10

Have a Seat

THIS ROOM was a junk room until we had a surprise overnight guest coming. I used a thrifted chair and dresser, layered a few small rugs, brought in a stump for a table, threw in a plant for some green, tacked up some white streamers for fun, and put a mattress on the floor with mixed neutral-colored patterned linens to create an instant guest room.

It's not about what it is,
it's about what it can become.

— DR. SEUSS, *THE LORAX*

Money-Saving Tips
for Furnishing Your Home

Once I gave myself permission to take my time, make mistakes, and be a savvy shopper, I was free to have fun with the process of creating a beautiful, meaningful room. If you look at furniture advertisements, you'll see phrases like "style you can afford now" and "no interest until 2045." If you looked only at advertising, you might assume that (1) everyone replaces an entire room all at one time on one day (and why not make it easy and do it all from one store?), and (2) it's impossible to pay cash to furnish a home.

There's nothing wrong with buying all your furniture for a room from Rooms to Go if you love that. On the other hand, if you loved the room (including furniture, side tables, pillows, rug, and lamps) you bought in the same transaction at Rooms to Go, you wouldn't be reading this book, right?

BEFORE

Many of us long for something more in our homes than a set of perfectly matching furniture. We long for meaningful beauty. But we don't know where to start, so sometimes it's easier to buy it all at once and be done with it already. And that works fine if it solves the problem and is logical and easy and finished and you love it. But often it leaves us unsettled because our home still doesn't represent our family or surround us with beauty.

My Favorite Makeovers in My House

Copper twin chairs that simply needed their arms and feet painted white, blue armoire that went from wood to blue, white TV dresser from French Provincial Little Girl to Glam, slipcovers that changed the whole sofa with $200 of fabric.

TOP Before: a pair of armchairs from the Salvation Army (forty dollars each)

ABOVE Before: eighteen-dollar yard-sale dresser

RIGHT After: much better after painting the wood on the chairs and the dresser with white paint and cleaning up a pair of thrifted glass lamps

There's another downside to buying everything for one room on the same day: you usually get sick of everything in five years on the very same day. What a horrible day that will be. Wouldn't it be easier to tweak things over time?

There are many ways to beat the system, which is why I'm going to devote a whole chapter to these money-saving tips. No one person needs to do all of these. Find one or two ideas that work for you and incorporate them into your home. Once you realize that the goal of your home isn't to falsely appear perfect, it becomes fun to create a pretty space even while on a tight budget.

Here are some of the ideas I've used in my home to avoid going into debt, starting fights with my husband, or feeling guilty for purchasing something. Even if I had all the money in the world, I'd still look for secondhand pieces for my home. No furniture store can replicate the depth of beauty and story that older pieces carry. Plus, even though we are no longer poor college students eating our bills and drinking fish-stick juice to stay alive, it's a priority for us to save and be generous.

> Even if I had all the money in the world, I'd still look for secondhand pieces for my home.

Furnishing a home in economical, creative ways is responsible and fun! So here we go.

Makeovers

Everyone has pieces of furniture in their home. Yes, I know it's all wrong and you hate half of it and the other half is worn out. The color is awful, the fabric is torn, the finish is gold or silver or whichever one "they" are telling us is out of style. Making something over is taking something you already have that you don't love and making it better.

Think about the furniture in your home that you love because of its sentimental value, function, or size, and consider whether there's something you can do to make it more your style. Maybe you can change out the knobs, buy a new lampshade, paint it, recover it, or embellish it in some way. Remember what we talked about in the risk chapter: start small and work your way to bigger makeovers. You can't ruin something you don't like.

DIY

So you see something beautiful that your friend recently hired out and you *love* it. But you can't afford the high price tag. You could totally do it yourself.

DIYs are often projects that we assume we need to hire out. But Google and YouTube offer great tutorials just a click away. Take baby steps and try one DIY:

- Paint your walls
- Rewire a lamp
- Board and batten a room
- Recover your dining room chairs
- Add a frame to your bathroom mirror

We added board and batten to my office. (Shhh, it was in a rental; here's to assuming the owners will love it as much as we do!) It was a weekend job that took awhile, but each step was simple.

SUNBURST mirror made
out of poster board

ONCE AGAIN, the twenty-dollar thrifted chair,
free stump table, and a pair of glass lamps I found
for eight dollars each at a thrift store. I rewired
one of the lamps and replaced the shades.

Hack It

So there's a certain something that you are in love with. An expensive pillow, a patchwork chair, an abstract painting, but you can't afford it. So you hack it. (I love that word. It sounds fun and evil at the same time.) You come up with a way to create the same type of thing by using shortcuts. Throughout this book you will find photographs of some of my favorite hacks: the sunburst mirror I made out of poster board, the duct-tape wall in our bedroom, which I can't seem to stop talking about, recycled yard-sale crystals that I hung on my chandelier, and Ikea embellished drapes.

Become Yard-Sale Stubborn

I cringe when I hear people say, "I *never* found anything at yard sales that one time I went." You can't find a great deal if you don't go. Yardsalers are a self-selecting group of people who are willing to get up early on a cold Saturday morning to park their cars in odd places at other people's houses, walk through wet grass, and paw through a bunch of old junk they don't want, then repeat up to twenty times in the hope of finding that amazing three-dollar treasure. It's not for everyone, but if you

stick with it, you'll usually be rewarded. Some
of my favorite yard-sale finds are the white table
I use in my office, which I bought for fifteen
dollars, the white dresser pictured a few pages
ago in the makeover section, and a library table.

Love Your Thrift Stores

My neighbor was over the other day and asked
if that blue dresser in my office was from Pottery
Barn. I proudly told her no, it was eighty-five
dollars from a thrift store, and then I painted it.
She then proclaimed one of the greatest myths
that we all have to get past: "I bet you find
something at thrift stores every time you go."

I find something worth buying only once
every ten times I go to a thrift store, if that.

To find great deals at thrift stores for things
that you can actually use, you have to be willing
to walk out empty-handed about 90 percent of
the time. This wasn't something I had time to
do when my boys were younger, but now I can
quickly run into two thrift stores in less than
twenty minutes. I can swing by once or twice a
week if I want.

There's a huge misconception that people
who find things at thrift stores somehow have
great ability to see things others can't. People
who find great things at thrift stores are long-
suffering more than they are visionaries. For
some reason we have the ability to enter a thrift
store time and time again, passing by the same
dirty crutches and water-stained particleboard
desk each time, to see if anything new has come
in since we were there last. Really, it's more
stubborn tenacity than anything else.

VINTAGE SAILFISH: a $350 splurge of all splurges found on Craigslist

Take Advantage of Craigslist

Craigslist is not full of killers. Some of the best deals can be found on this the most generic of websites. It's not for the faint of heart. You have to be diligent and pore through lots of stuff you don't want and put up with people who thought they could sell a piece of furniture without posting a little thing like a photo.

I turned to Craigslist when I wanted two specific things for our home. One was a sailfish. I grew up looking at a sailfish on my grandparents' wall, so I have fond memories of a dead taxidermied fish. (The fact that a mounted sailfish makes me happy is a lesson unto itself. Children associate memories with just about anything. It doesn't have to be fantastic or beautiful. This theory also explains why I absolutely love the smell of cigarette smoke. I don't smoke, but I rarely mind it when others do, because the smell takes me back to good times with grandparents. But I digress.)

Anyway, Craigslist makes you work for the deal, but if you are willing to email back and forth a little and drive somewhere with a friend (I said it's not *full* of killers, not that there are *no* killers) knowing you could hate what you see, you can find some really nice things. As you are searching around on Craigslist, be sure to use all types of words to find what you want. If you are looking for a Chesterfield sofa, you'll need to search "couch," "love seat," and "tufted." You have to think like a seller who may not know or care about what an item is usually called.

THE EVER-CHANGING
family room

Repurpose

We need to stop stereotyping furniture. Dressers aren't just for bedrooms anymore. They *love* being used in the kitchen, in the hall, on the long wall in the entry, under television sets, in the closet, and even in the bathroom. You've probably seen doors hung on the wall and used for headboards, but all pieces of furniture like to be used in unusual ways.

Use a pair of side chairs at the end of your formal dining table. Put a sofa table at the end of your bed. Hang a rug on the wall.

Barter

I'm sure that you know people who have skills you don't have. Those people think you have skills too. Maybe you are an accountant and would be willing to do your painter's taxes in exchange for painting your two-story foyer and family room. Maybe you pet-sit your friend's dog while your friend is out of the country, and in exchange she reupholsters a chair for you because she's a skilled upholsterer. There are many

A BIFOLD DOOR hung sideways under the bar to protect the wall from three boys' dirty bare feet

ways to barter items and skills when you don't have cash. Years ago I fluffed and staged a friend's house in exchange for some delicious home-cooked dinners.

My friend Happy Patterned Angela is a patient artist who has painted and sold countless pieces of furniture. There are few things in our home that get more everyday wear than our coffee table, so when I found a fifteen-dollar table with a questionable finish at a thrift store, I asked her to paint it for me, and promised that later I'd do something for her. I'm usually up for painting furniture myself, but the finish on this one seemed tricky and I was still practicing my furniture painting skills. It turned out amazing.

THIRTY-DOLLAR library table from a yard sale

(Although now that I think about it, I'm pretty sure I still owe her a favor.)

One of my favorite people to barter with is myself. You don't even have to have multiple personalities to pull it off. A few years ago, my husband wanted a new TV. At the time, we had a huge cube TV from the 1600s, so I knew he was right — it was probably time for an upgrade, and really, he doesn't ask for much. But we didn't want to blow our budget, so we made a deal with ourselves. We paid cash for the TV in January, but canceled cable for half the year until we recouped the cost of the TV. It worked like a charm, and at the end of the year, it felt like we got a TV for free.

Sometimes bartering comes in the form of giving something a good home. My mom and I were out yardsaling one day and found that eye-catching old library table I told you about a few pages ago. I loved it. And so did the owner of the table. Her grandfather had found it years earlier in a building he owned. The ninety-dollar price tag on the table was too much for me, so we left. A few hours later, my mom surprised me with the table. She paid thirty dollars for it. Turns out that the seller was really looking for someone who would love the table as much as she loved it. My mom successfully convinced her that the table would be in great hands at my house.

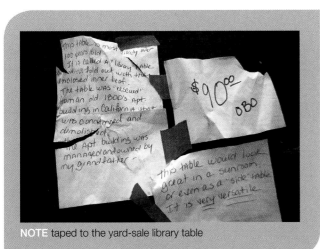

NOTE taped to the yard-sale library table

TOP I took this photo and knew I didn't like the clock right there, so I moved it back where it was.

BOTTOM One of these garden stools was $150, and one was $25. Can you tell which is which?

Become a Picker

Have the mindset of Frank and Mike from the TV show *American Pickers*. They are always on the lookout for a good pick, even if they are simply on their way to eat dinner. When you are in house-primping mode, allow yourself to notice all things house-y. Your brain will do this for you. Be attentive to anything you could possibly use in your home. So whether you are in your parents' attic or the old shed at your friend's house, driving by the pile of furniture that your neighbors left behind on the side of the road when they moved, or dropping off stuff at the dump, if you see something that you think could work in your home, ask about using it. Be always on the prowl for finds.

Move Stuff Around

Moving furniture is one of my favorite ways to feel like I'm getting fresh stuff. It's such a thrill to try out the little-used dresser from the guest room in the foyer and figure out that it looks great there. It's the closest thing to getting free stuff.

For an entire year, I was sure my sofa would look hideous in the corner of the room. Finally I decided to move it there "just to see." After eight minutes of moving stuff around, a broken fingernail, and some sweaty pits, I figured out that the corner was the exact place our sofa needed to be. I had measured, pictured it in my head, and asked friends, and all those things had pointed

to the sofa in the corner being a bad idea. It wasn't until I moved it that I realized it was perfect.

It takes only a few minutes to move something. You can always move it back and no one needs to know. Move your stuff! It's the free-est, riskless-iest thing you can do in your home.

And if you are paying attention to the photos in this book, my moving-stuff-around ways are obvious.

Shop the House

Shopping the House is the fun little sister to Moving Stuff. When you shop the house, put yourself in the mindset of a person who doesn't live in your house. Pretend you are a distinguished designer, if that helps. Walk around your home and look at every room as if you were shopping at a store where everything is free.

> Tip: when you move your furniture around "just to see," snap a few photos. Sometimes seeing a room through a camera lens helps you better see how the layout works for your family.

Say you walk into your bedroom and there is a lamp that's been there for years — so long you hardly even see it anymore. Don't tell yourself you can't use it in the family room because it's fine in your bedroom. No. You tell yourself that you want to find the best possible place for that lamp, right now in your home, and that it might not be your bedroom. As you shop the house, you are open to trying any item in any room in order to have the best placements of all your pretty things. Shopping the house is one of my favorite parts of creating a pretty home.

I know what you are wondering: Doesn't that mean that everything in my house is always up for grabs and could be constantly rotating? Yes! Isn't that fun?! But it doesn't have to mean that. Simply put, you want everything in your home to be in the best possible spot; once you find that spot, you can relax, unless you are purchasing new things all the time.

I like to use the priority system to help me find the best place for everything.

Walk around your home and identify the most important wall in each room. Often it's the wall you see first when you walk into a room. In our family room, the most important wall is the tiny fireplace wall. Even though it's the smallest wall in the room, it's the one you see from most other rooms and the wall directly across from the main entrance. If that wall isn't right, then the whole room is off.

So as I shop the house looking for items for a particular room, the most important wall gets priority in that room. If I have a piece of artwork that looks great both on the fireplace wall and on a secondary wall, guess which wall gets dibs? The fireplace wall, because he's more important.

You can do this with the entire house. If you have a mirror that looks good in both the guest room and the foyer, you get to decide which room needs it most. It may mean that you take down the mirror from a place where it's been for years and looks pretty good to put it in a place where it looks stunning.

This doesn't just apply to walls — you can prioritize rooms, or sometimes an event or a season of your life becomes a priority. If you have a guest for the summer, then being able to accommodate them could be a priority. If you are expecting a new baby, then quickly completing the nursery could be your priority. There's no right or wrong priority; you get to decide, and then you can choose what to use where.

Move away from thinking each item has only one place in your home. Most items in your home would look great in multiple rooms; it's your job to find the best place for each piece.

MisTreat Your Windows

After I learned about the wonderful world of window treatments and all the options and customizations available, I made it my goal that one day I too would be the owner of custom window treatments complete with silk fabric that I picked out myself. The time came about eight years ago in Our Imperfect Average Dream House when my husband and I decided to fix up our family room. We ordered a new sofa (in the next chapter we'll talk about where to splurge and where to save), and I found a rug. Next on my list were the window treatments.

> We all have our indulgences, but apparently window treatments aren't mine.

I bought enough silk to cover the windows. I had a friend who was a designer with access to a workroom, a magical place where expert sewers do custom needlework on soft goods for designers (that's fancy talk for sewing drapes and cushions and bedspreads in the fabric you and your designer choose), and I was going to ask her to help me make sure they were made to the proper specifications. These drapes were going to make my windows look like a million bucks!

I brought the fabric home and set the bolt up next to my window to try to get a feel for what it would look like. It was kind of hard to picture it, so I unwound a length of fabric to drape over the rod that was already up — long enough to reach the floor. Oh, that was more like it! I could see that these window treatments were going to be fabulous.

I'm nothing if not impatient, so I decided that since I bought a little extra yardage, it couldn't hurt anything for me to go ahead and cut four lengths of fabric out of the silk I purchased. The workroom staff would probably thank me for saving them a step.

RAW FABRIC folded and clipped onto drapery clip rings that hang on a curtain rod. No sewing!

DRAPERY clip rings. Look for them in the drapery hardware aisle.

HEM TAPE

MUCH-LOVED glue gun

Not only did we already have rods installed, they came complete with clip-on rings. So hey, I figured I could go ahead and clip up my four pieces of silk fabric real quick, just to see what they would look like. After clipping the fabric pieces up, I folded the edges back so I could get a better look. Within about five minutes of tweaking the fabric, I could totally tell these window treatments would look fantastic when they were done. I liked them so much, I kept the fabric pieces up for a few days.

And then my designer friend came over. The first words out of her mouth? "I love your window treatments. You already finished them!" I took her over and showed her the raw edges, the unlined, unhemmed, unfelted, unweighted hastily cut fabric, and she mentioned that they looked almost like the real thing. We both had a good laugh.

She left that day and I looked long and hard at my windows. She was right; they did look almost finished. The truth was, they looked 90 percent as good as the finished product. But I still needed to pay for the linings and interlining and labor; I wasn't even 50 percent done with paying out money for these drapes to have them professionally finished. And even though we had the money, I couldn't bring myself to spend it just to get that last 10 percent finished. And that is how Window MisTreatments came about.

Since that day, I've been okay with good enough on my windows. We all have our indulgences, but apparently window treatments aren't mine. On my windows are either raw-edged pieces of fabric clipped up, inexpensive white bedsheets, or if I'm in an especially fancy mood, Ikea drapes. Every house we've lived in since I started MisTreating my windows has had blinds, so the window treatments are purely decorative anyway. If the kind of people who come into my home are going to walk up to my window treatments, turn them over, and inspect them, and then decide that I'm not worthy of their friendship, I'm good with that. They did us both a favor. Maybe I should introduce every potential friend to my Window MisTreatments as a litmus test.

Take Advantage of Nature

Branches, stumps, moss, feathers, nests, and beautiful rocks are readily available for your decorating pleasure. I've even been known to cut weeds from down by the little creek in our back yard. Shucks, I've even pulled over on the side of the road to cut some wildflowers. I've also walked into a business and asked if I could pay them for some hydrangeas that were growing on their bushes outside their shop. (No one's ever accepted the money yet.) One of the most beautiful center-pieces you will see is a simple tree branch cut and put in a vase.

We currently have nine stump tables in our home. Yes, real stumps. Yes, I am addicted. It started with a beloved fallen tree from the back yard, and now friends and neighbors bring me stumps. Stumps are God's side tables. Like snowflakes, no two are alike. Unlike snowflakes, you can bring them into your home and enjoy them.

I love stumps because all you need is a chainsaw (or if your friends bring you stumps, often they are already cut to a size you can use) and time and sandpaper and maybe paint, and you can create a side table. I'm not a stump specialist, but you'll get better, less buggy results if you let the stump sit in your garage or a shed for about a year so all the litter critters can work their way out. There are lots of ways to de-critterfy and seal your stump, and since I'm not a stump specialist, for the second time in this book I will tell you to Google it. Don't you love paying for a book and then being told to "just Google it"? After that you can debark it (if you want) and sand it (super rewarding) and leave it, stain it, paint it, or even put casters on it. I even carved our initials in one.

Author not responsible if you bring in a stump full of termites. Stump it up at your own risk.

Pay Attention to Sale Sites

Couponers have gained a lot of attention recently with their savvy stacking of coupons at the grocery store. But we furniture shoppers can be savvy too. Sites like Groupon and flash-sale sites like One Kings Lane, Joss and Main, and Zulily offer great daily deals on furniture and items for your home. Just like with regular shopping, you can't assume everything is the best deal available, but with a little Googling (there I go again) of the item, you can quickly tell whether what you are looking at is the best price. Plus, if you are active in social media like Facebook, you can tell your friends about what you purchased, use a referral code that the sales site provides, and over time earn store credits if your friends decide to make a purchase. It's a win-win.

> Once we stop insisting on perfection, we are free to purchase things that aren't perfect.

One marvelous day, the stars aligned and I had a $10 credit from Groupon for referring a friend. I applied that to the purchase of a Groupon for a $30 store credit to One Kings Lane — the store credit was on sale at Groupon for $15. Stay with me. I paid out of pocket $5 for a $30 credit for One Kings Lane, where I also had a $15 credit from referring a friend. So I was able to purchase $45 worth of something for my home from One Kings Lane for just $5. Playing the game isn't for everyone, but some of us think that kind of challenge is fun.

Patiently Befriend the Trends

Usually when an item becomes all the rage (as the kids say), you can count on its getting replicated by even the least expensive stores within a few years. Target has made an art out of providing trendy goods for a fraction of the price shortly after they become popular.

Here's a recent example from my house: a few years back, garden stools were in practically every magazine photograph. Within a year, you could find what started out as a $150 investment for twenty dollars at local discount stores.

Often trends are actually timeless. Garden stools aren't a new invention. Neither are the floor poufs that were so popular a few years ago. I bought a new pouf because clearly I haven't broken free from being a slave to the trends, but I also found a vintage pouf for eight dollars secondhand. If you are willing to shop around, many times you can find older versions of currently trending items.

A PAIR of poufs

ANGELA'S FOYER

Become an Imperfectionist

Once we stop insisting on perfection, we are free to purchase things that aren't perfect.

I wanted a cowhide rug for years, but didn't want to dish out the hundreds of dollars that they cost. One day at a flea market, I found a beautiful cowhide rug for sixty dollars. The only problem? It was missing a limb. I didn't care; this was my chance to own a cowhide, and I knew I'd be tucking part of it under a piece of furniture anyway.

My friend Happy Patterned Angela has learned the subtle art and value of working with imperfections. Her home is layered and storied and cozy because she's willing to purchase the secondhand, cast-off quilt with a rip in it. She'll then make it into a pillow and a few handbags. Got an old scrap of fabric with a stain on it? That's not trash. To Angela, it's the perfect thing to be featured in an embroidery hoop.

ANGELA PROVES you can mix all sorts of fabrics.

Marry Furniture

Do you know that if you paint two pieces of any type of furniture the same color, they look like they are related? Paint a pair of bookshelves and a dresser all the same color, flank the dresser with the shelves, and ta-da, you have a custom television unit complete with shelving. Mirrors and mismatched dressers are great candidates for marriage, as are tables and inexpensive bookcases stacked on them like a hutch.

Contrary to what furniture stores would like us to believe, there are lots of ways to furnish a home. Brand new is a wonderful option, but made-over and slipcovered or painted can be just as beautiful, sometimes even better than new.

BEFORE

AFTER Small chest and tall mirror bought at two different times from two different stores are now united as one with a little white paint.

CHAPTER 11

When a Room Doesn't Look Quite Right

Great things are done by a series of small things brought together.

— VINCENT VAN GOGH

Small Tweaks That Make a Big Difference

If you are looking at a space and feel like something isn't quite right or that it's unfinished, maybe one of these tweaks can help. These are not rules. For every rule, tip, and trick, there is someone out there breaking said rule or tip or trick beautifully. But these ideas have worked their way into my home, and they might make a difference in yours. If you want extra inspiration, flip back through the book for a second look at photos that show examples of all of these ideas.

Lamps

A well-placed lamp can be worth its weight in Target gift cards. Beautiful, warm, filtered lamplight has the power to create little halos of light around all who enter to sit and relax.

Have you ever walked into a home at night and all the overhead lights of the devil are on and you feel like you are either shopping in a warehouse or being interrogated at the police station? Overhead lights do us no favors. They age us and give a room a hospital-waiting-room feel. Lamps are our friends.

Lamps don't have to cost a fortune — some of my favorite lamps are secondhand. Also, HomeGoods seems to have a never-ending plethora of twenty- to forty-dollar lamps.

An interesting lamp base can double as a piece of art with its shape, material, and size, and a well-placed lamp can take away the need for much else on a table. So splurging on a lamp that gives you both light and design can add great value to the function and form of a space.

Rugs

If you feel like your space is disjointed, it might be because your rug is too small. Your furniture deserves to have at least its front feet on the rug.

For years, I made the mistake of putting a five-by-eight rug where an eight-by-ten rug needed to go. Bigger rugs cost more and are a pain to put in the car. I always wanted to make a smaller rug work where I really needed a large rug. But 'tis better to go rugless for a few more months while you save for the correct size for a room than to hastily buy a rug that you'll sell on Craigslist for half-price in six months.

A well-made rug can be an investment that you keep for a long time. A bigger rug will make the room feel larger, cushier, and more beautiful.

Plants

I'm still surprised at the power green plants have to finish off a room. Do plants tend to die on you? Think of it this way: purchasing a house plant for $6.99 and keeping it alive for eighteen months does not mean you failed; it means that you got to enjoy a beautiful plant in your home for less than a penny and a half a day. That's a bargain!

A plant is always the first thing to catch my eye when I enter a room. Want to see the impact that plants have in a space? Open up a shelter magazine and count the number of plants and flowers. Imagine each room without the plants. Would it have the same feel? Plants bring life to a room.

Natural Light

Watch any episode of *House Hunters* on HGTV and you'd think that we are starved for natural light — and we are. The hunters of the houses always, without fail, comment on the natural light or lack thereof in a home. And then most of the time, once they buy their homes with the lovely large windows, what do they do? Cover them up.

Natural light is a free design gift from God. Don't waste it. Hang your drapes so that they cover the wall next to the window and just a few inches of the window, not so they cover all the light of the window with a few precious inches in the middle for the rays to fight their way through into your home. It's fine to close your drapes when you want privacy, but don't take away your option to soak up every inch of the natural light you purchased when you bought the house.

> Natural light is a free design gift from God.

If you have heavy curtains covering your windows, consider purchasing longer curtain rods so that you can open wide the drapes and let the natural light come in. And you get a bonus: hanging your drapes over the wall makes your windows appear much larger. Another design trick is to hang your rods high, close to the ceiling. It opens the room and makes it seem larger to have your drapes majestically hanging from on high.

This is now the first thing I do whenever we move to a new house. The rods are almost always hung right at the top of the window and they only span the width of the window. I don't want to cover my windows with my drapes; I want to enhance the windows, so I do the work of getting larger rods and hanging them higher. It's always been worth it.

One more life-altering natural light tip is simply to open the blinds. Daily. If you really want to be risky, pull the blinds up to the top or, gasp, remove them. Your friends will ask you whether you just painted the room, it will look so fresh and sparkly. Every room looks better with natural light. Take advantage of it.

Use the Good Stuff

One of my design mentors, JoAnne Lenart-Weary, once said that putting a candle next to a lamp is redundant. Besides making me laugh, she also ruined me forever for putting two types of light sources next to each other regardless of how different they seem.

My personal pet peeve is an unlit candlewick. I know it seems odd to purchase something and then set it on fire. But never lighting your candles is like setting out cupcakes and then not eating one. *Why?* Candles are meant to be burned. They are not an endangered resource, so stop protecting them and dusting them; burn them and enjoy them. If not, let me have your candles (and cupcakes). I'll give them a good home where they can be used to their fullest potential and no longer neglected.

Lighting your candles probably isn't going to change your entire room. But it could help change your mindset. The beautiful things in your home are there for you to enjoy. Lighting the candles can be a baby step to fully enjoying your home. Next thing you know, you'll be unpacking the good dishes and using the guest towels.

Break Up the Sets

I know the furniture store sells the sofa with the love seat and the matching coffee and end tables. But it doesn't mean you have to buy the entire matching set. Most likely, all those rooms that you've pinned on Pinterest and bookmarked in magazines are not rooms made up of sets; instead they're layered with mixed woods and paints and styles and eras of furniture.

 If you feel like your family room or bedroom is lacking in personality, it could be because everything is a set. If you've already invested in a set, not to worry; we've all done it. Consider divorcing the set and putting the members in separate rooms. If you have two dressers, two side tables, a bed, and a mirror that are all part of a bedroom set and you feel stuck, pick a color and paint a few of the pieces to mix it up a little, change out some knobs, and trade the matching mirror for the sunburst mirror in the family room.

Pillow Talk

Are your decorative pillows flat? This is not the fault of your family, whom you've begged not to flatten your pillows. Maybe you are purchasing the wrong pillows to begin with. Look for feather inserts. Feathers, also known as God's stuffing, still create the most fluffable pillows.

 These days, you can usually purchase pillow covers separately (Etsy is my favorite pillow-cover buying place), so the inside of the pillow can be whatever you choose. I've been known to feel up all the pillows in a thrift store just to find the feather pillows so I can go home, tear off the ugly cover,

wash the insert in super hot water, and then put my own pillow cover on it. Feather pillows will continue to refluff after years of abuse. Remember, your throw pillows are there to serve you.

You Won't Hurt the Builder's Feelings

If you've ever been house shopping, you might have noticed that more often than not, the light fixtures in almost every home are sad and neglected. It's an honest mistake that I've made countless times. You buy a house, the overhead lighting is there and seems adequate, and you simply never think about it. But just because a builder bought a hundred identical, functional overhead lights doesn't mean that's the best choice of lighting in your spaces.

> Overhead lighting is a huge opportunity to add personality and style to your spaces.

Don't let the expense hold you back. The eye-catching overhead lantern in our room was a thirty-dollar secondhand find, probably less than the cost of the ceiling fan that was there before. We weren't desperate for a fan in our room, but if we were, I'd simply use a vintage-style tabletop fan.

Don't forget about your chandeliers. I once heard someone say, "There's no such thing as a chandelier that's too big for a room." I'm not sure I completely agree with that, but I admit I've yet to see a chandelier too big for a room. Most of the time, we buy our chandeliers too small. When in doubt, go a size or two up.

The builder shouldn't get to choose what chandelier looks best over your dining room table; you get to decide. Overhead lighting is a huge opportunity to add personality and style to your spaces. Plus, if and when you sell your home, it makes it look upgraded and customized.

Splurges and Steals

One of the most common questions I'm asked is what items I think are worth spending good money on, and what I try to find for less. Clearly my cheapness precedes me. So here's a loosely held list of things that I'm apt to dish out more cash for:

Beds and sheets. Well-made beds and high-thread-count sheets, because we spend a good percentage of our lives in and on them.

Rugs. Rugs because we walk on them. They are one of the things in our home that we treat the worst. Rugs also, from a design perspective, work hard, setting the tone of the whole room. So they are worth dishing out some cash for. Don't forget to buy big!

Sofas. Sofas because they need to last, and they need to be a place to snuggle a sick child, cozy up for a movie, pray with friends, and squeeze a lot of people onto. They are the workhorse of a home (besides the toilet of course, but let's skip that one).

Decorating as a Renter

If you're a renter, focus on things you can take with you to the next house. Furniture, lamps, and rugs all make a big impact in a space. Drapes and pattern can also help fill up a room. As far as furniture goes, purchase items that could work in multiple rooms in any house you live in. You already know how much I love dressers, small tables, and side chairs that can work almost anywhere. I never regret buying them.

If you know you're going to be in a place for only a year, do a mad dash of decorating as soon as you move in. Invite your mom or a friend to help you unpack and immediately put things on the wall. If you wait three months, then 25 percent of the time you live there will be with your stuff on the floor waiting to be put up. That's not fun.

On the other hand, a year isn't worth fretting much over bad carpet or ugly colors. You can deal with those things for a year. Consider it a sabbatical from having to purchase anything that stays on the home's person. It's a nice break not to have to buy new knobs or perennials or pine straw or paint. Enjoy it and invest in things you can take with you.

If I know we are going to be renting for more than a year, the one change that is most worth making is the overhead lighting. Save the boring/ugly/hated-for-whatever-reason lighting that you take down so you can put it back before you move out. But putting up a stunning chandelier that you love (and can take with you when you move) can change the whole mood of a room. We've changed out the overhead lighting in three-quarters of the rooms in our current rental. It takes about twenty minutes per fixture and makes the house feel like our home.

Signature pieces. Meaningful signature pieces, like my sailfish, can make a home. I'd rather pay to frame something that my children made than pay for a mass-produced piece of art that all my neighbors have. Amen.

Light fixtures. One or two special light fixtures make a big difference. If I'm really attached to them and we are getting ready to list our home for sale, I'll switch them out with something less expensive so I can take them with me. Don't underestimate the impact that a big special chandelier can have on a room.

Then there are some things that in a perfect world I'd love to get to buy new off the rack, but I can find them for much less money if I'm patient. The things I give myself time to purchase because they are easy to find and inexpensive secondhand are:

Side chairs. Side chairs are easy to find at a thrift store or yard sale. Even if they need a coat of paint or fresh upholstery, you still come out paying much less than buying new. Plus, sometimes because the price is so good, you'll be tempted to purchase something that's a little risky and that can turn out to be a great addition to your home.

Small tables and desks. Believe me. They are everywhere and can be easily changed with a quick coat of paint.

Dressers. I have eight dressers in my house. Three I purchased new; five I purchased used. My favorite dresser is the one I bought for eighteen dollars at a yard sale.

Wall art. I am allergic to mass-produced wall art. There's simply no need to buy a cheaply framed, glassed-over something to put on your walls. I'm a big believer in creating your own art, but if you aren't ready for that, mirrors are one of the best-kept secrets of secondhand shopping. They are easy to paint over, look pretty in any room, and make the room look bigger.

My friend Happy Patterned Angela wins the award for most original art for the least amount of money. Until I met her, I never even considered looking through the wall-art section of the thrift stores. Her home is filled with original paintings that somehow all look great together.

ANGELA'S thrifted painting collection

Accessories. Accessories are the first and easiest thing to change out when a room seems tired. I'm a sucker for trends, and I get the catalogs from the latest and greatest furniture stores. From time to time, I splurge on a special accessory, but oftentimes I can find similar items for much less secondhand. So be aware of what accessories you like, but be open to finding them in random places.

Candles. I love finding all sorts of colorful candles secondhand. They are usually unlit and pristine because America thinks we have a candle shortage and hardly anyone ever lights their candles. More candles for us!

On Buying

Don't buy things to go with stuff you hate. The Rental Where It Was Worth Losing Our Deposit had a kitchen that was the standby for nightmare rentals everywhere: avocado green and orange. It also boasted dark paneling. So I thought I could help things by purchasing some green and orange dishes that I thought were okay. They weren't my style at all. I hated the colors, but I thought maybe they would make me like the room better. All they did was waste my money.

CHAPTER 12

House to Home

IT'S A SICKNESS. I cannot leave this wall alone. It's too fun to play with it and change it up!

The home should be the
Treasure chest of living.

— LE CORBUSIER

Those Quirky Finishing Touches

Now we arrive at the finishing touches that separate the model homes from the lived-in, loved-on homes. These are my tips from the inner chamber, tips from the heart, tips you might laugh at, tips that have defined my personal style. Over the years, I've come to be a lot more lenient with myself and where we live. Here's how.

Everyday on Display

Years ago when we lived in The Apartment I Thought I Was Too Good For and had negative ten dollars to our names every month, I asked for beautiful everyday items for Christmas and my birthday. I wanted the pretty soap dispenser, Kleenex cover, and salad bowl. I figured if I needed these things anyway, if these things were going to be visible in my home, and if people wanted to get me something, why not make them beautiful and functional? Instead of buying myself a cheap, ugly plastic cutting board, I bought a wooden cutting board so that I would enjoy seeing it on my counter.

As often as possible, I try to get double miles out of everyday objects, and I evaluate almost everything that comes into our home to see if I can display it somewhere. I probably take that philosophy entirely too far. But I can't stand for my bracelets and necklaces to be packed away out of sight when I'm not wearing them. They are beautiful, and I want to enjoy them every day, so in our bedroom I have on

display a large tray full of bracelets, and a bust who doesn't mind wearing chunky necklaces. I've also figured out that I need beautiful bowls conveniently placed around our home for keeping my bracelets, my nail polish, and glasses the boys removed from their faces.

Every Christmas, I get out some little woolen winter hats that our boys used to wear and hang them on the antlers or the coatrack or set them on a shelf — just tiny, meaningful mementos that have a second life as decorations.

Pot racks are another example of everyday on display. We've had pot racks in a few homes, and they're a great reminder to spend two dollars more on the pot that looks good. With all of our pretty, functional pots hanging in our kitchen, I don't need to do much decorating in that room.

I finally bought a nice boot tray. Unlike in the magazine pictures that show boot trays holding exactly two pairs of boots — one perfectly clean pair of shiny black Hunter Wellies and one perfectly clean pair of cowboy boots — our tray is sometimes disheveled and holds a dog leash and dirty Converse. But there's something about grouping things in a beautiful container that somehow makes them look pretty.

If I have a bag, scarf, or jacket that's on the nicer side, instead of hiding it away, I'll hang it someplace obvious so it can add to the decor. It's kind of a two-for — I get to use it, and on its off days, it gets to be a decoration.

- Straight and curvy lines
- Masculine and feminine
- Black and white
- Rustic and glitzy
- Matte and glossy
- Vintage and modern
- Large and small
- Geometric and organic
- Patterned and solid

OPPOSITES I even used the idea of opposites in my Christmas decorating this year: shiny copper metals and matte paper showflakes, white doilies on black paper, geometric boxes with curvy finger-knitted garland.

Opposites Attract

One of the least talked about tricks of the design world is working with opposites. Most finished rooms that you drool over on Pinterest and in magazines have incorporated this trick, and it can make a room have that "collected over time" look that people are too impatient to wait for. On the other hand, when you look at flyers from the big-box furniture stores, you can immediately tell that it's not a real house. One of the reasons is the lack of opposites.

Incorporating opposites completes and balances a room. Sometimes it happens automatically; sometimes you need to look for that visual harmony that opposites provide.

You don't need every kind of opposite in every room, and you probably already have some in each room of your house. But if you feel like a space is missing something, consider adding in some opposites.

Shop the house and incorporate things you already have into a gallery wall:

- Consider using objects with different dimensions instead of all flat, one-inch-thick frames.
- Look for items that aren't covered with glass. When everything is under glass, it feels untouchable and looks glaring.
- Pick a few colors and stick with them.
- Mix straight edges with curved.
- Consider adding one circular item. This can change the entire mood of a gallery wall.
- Start with black-and-white photos. Once you are confident in building gallery walls, work with color photos.
- Rule nothing out until you try it on the wall.
- Use a shelf or sconce to lean one frame on for interest.
- Don't use all photos. Mix it up with framed kids art and paintings.
- Or do the opposite and choose a theme: all maps, all mirrors, all black-and-white photos, all finger paintings, all paint-by-number pictures.

TOP Every so often I paint over some old canvases with craft paint in the colors I'm currently crushing on.

BOTTOM Friends often comment on the accessories that our head planter is wearing. They tend to change every few weeks.

Paint It with Craft Paint

Every so often I paint over some old canvases with craft paint in the colors I'm currently crushing on.

My style and tastes have changed over the years, and so has my color palette. Instead of buying all new things to go with each new me, I just change the paint color.

We've already talked about painting furniture, but I'm talking about smaller things too. I always keep a drawer of craft paint handy for when something needs a quick color change. I've painted picture frames and their mats (don't buy new ones, paint the old!) and all manner of tchotchkes.

One of my favorite tricks is to change my wall art just by dumping my current colors on a canvas. I'll grab big paint cans of my current wall colors and some craft paint and spread them around and spatter them until it looks perfectly imperfect. My large forty-dollar canvas from a craft store has been painted four different times over the years. Not only does it add a touch of modern to your home, but you can do it with the kids.

Don't Keep a Journal, Keep a Gallery Wall

Every home could benefit from a gallery wall. Gallery walls are like family journals on display. They are easy to create and fun because you can change things out over time so they grow with you. I love gallery walls because there is no wrong way to do them. The crazier they look, the more exotic you appear. (Fancy folks call that being flamboyant.)

Find a Signature Piece

I always wanted to be one of those women who has a delicious signature dish that everyone requests when we attend get-togethers. I'm still searching for that dish as I volunteer to bring the two-liter drinks, but I do have some signature pieces in our home. They are the show-offs, the big shots, the attention-getting items that all of the other pieces in the room are jealous of. If the signature pieces were removed, our home would have less oomph. I like oomph. Oomph can make your entire space remarkable.

A signature piece could be a piece of furniture, artwork, a focal wall, or an architectural element like an oversized window. It could be a collection or something everyone has that is presented in a different way, like a stair rail painted hot pink. The signature piece in our home is the sailfish.

Not every room needs to have one large outspoken piece, but I do think every room should have one memorable item. If someone is trying to explain the room to a group of friends, they'd say, "Oh, it's the room with the huge stuffed buffalo." Enough said, we all know what room that is.

For example, our bedroom has the diamond duct-tape wall. The guest room has the white paper streamers; the front room has the random plate wall; our breakfast area has the extra-large chandelier; the bonus room has the basket-weave light fixture. The boys' rooms have the beautiful mess, just like my room did when I was their age.

It's not about finding an expensive item. It's about displaying an interesting item that you love. Sometimes a signature piece is the starting point of decorating a room, but I've discovered that it's usually something I've found close to the end of creating a room. Which, by the way, never actually ends.

Find Your Finishing Touch

Have you ever walked into the home of friends and immediately thought, *This house is so them*? Something about the home speaks volumes about the people who live there.

Happy Pattern Angela's finishing touch is layers and pattern. My friend Tracy's finishing touch is plants; she's the plant whisperer.

My finishing touch is quirk. The first time my friend Christina, a talented designer who values authenticity, came to my house, she looked around smiling and declared, "Everything is just a little bit off." She had no idea what a huge compliment that was to me, a person whose biggest fear (besides becoming a hoarder or becoming one of those people on the show *Oddities*) is for her house to look store-bought. For me, having things "off" is a sign that I'm embracing imperfection. Mission accomplished. Best compliment ever. I'm crazy. Or else a genius. It doesn't matter, does it? Because I love my house.

Adding Quirk

Anthropologie is one of my favorite stores. Not because of their clothes or dishes or wonderful-smelling candles. Those are all fabulous, but what I can't get enough of are the displays. Before you even walk into the store, you are greeted by a window display that at first glance is beautiful. Then it becomes striking, mesmerizing, and hypnotizing. As you look closer, you realize it's the materials they use that make it interesting. Anthropologie has learned the art of using everyday items in astounding and unique ways. They get stunning results because of the sheer number and repetition of items and the playful way they create these displays. If there are window displays in heaven, the designers responsible for the Anthropologie displays will be in charge of them.

THIS PLATE WALL grew over time. Old plates, dollar-store plates, and second-hand plates are hung with wire plate-hangers and layered simply by using some longer nails.

It's not about finding an expensive item.
It's about displaying an interesting
item that you love.

HANDMADE GARLAND made from cutting book pages into leaf shapes and gluing them together.

A few years ago, after I had a newly white-slipcovered sofa and my walls were blank slates, I walked into Anthropologie to secretly rub up against the displays and lust after the walls of tissue-paper flowers, bottle-cap art, and imperfectly framed ripped vintage paintings. I wondered if I could incorporate some of the Anthro feel into my home. I decided my home needed a little more playfulness, a little less run-of-the-mill. Being in Anthropologie made me feel like I was in elementary art class again. I loved art class. Only now I'm an adult. Instead of construction paper in primary colors, I wanted to mix beautiful everyday textures with my cottage furniture and thrift-store finds. I wondered if I could introduce something unexpected yet beautiful and not become that creepy woman down the street who puts mannequin heads in her house.

I decided my home needed artistic quirk. It happened over time, but looking back, I see now that quirk was a turning point for me. Once I added quirk, I fell deeply in love with my home. If I were better with words and more touchy-feely and smarter, I'd be able to pinpoint why. All I know is, once I allowed myself to be playful in my home, I enjoyed it more than ever. Adding quirky, whimsical, lighthearted, purposeless items in my home started a love affair that I can't shake. I feel like I'm back in art class, only I don't have to wait for Mrs. Barnhorst to explain what we are making.

Quirk is that last squeeze of lemon on the sautéed mushrooms, the zest of my home. Quirk brought me back to childhood, because I realized that the home I always dreamed of wasn't one that was sophisticated and completely grown-up, perfectly put together and classified as French Country or English Cottage or (gasp!) Modern. The home I longed for was one in which I was completely free to do what I wanted no matter what others might think. By allowing myself to add quirk, I was announcing to the world that — guess what? — I now have the confidence to put something in my home even though I know someone will think it's ridiculous. Once you experince that kind of freedom in decorating, you'll never go back, and your house will finally look the way you've always dreamed.

> The home I longed for was one in which I was completely free to do what I wanted no matter what others might think.

Here are three ways I added quirk to my home:

1. I decided to display my average items in un-average ways. For example, I've always had a wall of white plates, but this time I hung the plates in a whimsical manner. The decorative busts in our home hold plants and antlers and feathers and necklaces and clown noses and masks and hats, all depending on our mood and the season.

2. I used unexpected, disposable items in an expected way. What? Isn't that the opposite of what I just said? Yes! I experimented with creating wreaths out of plastic spoons. (I know you just rolled your eyes; I'm good with that.) Oh, and pom-poms. (It's okay; you don't have to understand.) I made a sunburst mirror out of poster board. With the help of friends, we created dozens of decorations with book pages for my sister's book-signing party, and then kept them up as decorations — for years. They are still up now as I type.

3. I decided to display things that made me happy even if they were a little odd. Things that were fun. Things that didn't have much purpose. And I *loved* it! Sailfish on the wall — check. A huge empty canvas leaning on the wall when my life seems hectic — yes. A three-armed cowhide rug — why not? A disco ball that reflects light all over the house — who wouldn't love that?

The unusual, quirky pieces in our home seem to whisper, *This is a place to have fun. This is a place where you don't have to take yourself too seriously. This is a place to be who you are.* Oh, how I've longed to hear that.

For me, adding that unexpected dash of quirk was the final nail in the coffin of pleasing others and caring about their opinion of my home. I've crossed over. I'm not decorating to please anyone else but me and my family, and it is wonderful.

Something funny happened once I gave up on creating the perfect, everyone-approved home. Shelter magazines started contacting me, wanting to feature our spaces in their magazines. It's not everyone's goal to be in a magazine, and I'm not saying that's the natural result of adding quirk. But what I am saying is that once I was free to be me in my home, I created a home that I loved, was proud of, and that others recognized as something special. It's like reverse home psychology.

Look Back

Different homes and different families call for different finishing touches. One way to find your finishing touch is to think back to your childhood. What decorative item filled you with wonder or made you happy?

For instance, I always *loved* birthday parties as a kid. Not for the chatty friends or the pink gifts or the piñatas filled with

TOP I created this "balloon-dalier" by tying balloons onto a little chandelier. (I taped the light switch off while they were up.) I was hosting a girls' weekend, and these inexpensive balloons made a huge impact in the space.

BOTTOM A bust planter sporting a pair of pink shades

candy but for the decorations, of course! One of the quirky things in my home are small happy decorations that I've allowed myself to leave up during every season. Streamers, masks, party hats, and pennants have all worked their way into my everyday design. It makes me happy!

Maybe for you, that finishing touch is to incorporate your favorite color, or always to have fresh flowers, or finally to frame and display all those black-and-white family photos. Whatever that thing is, I hope you find it. Or rather, I hope you pay attention to the simple pleasures that you enjoy, and choose to add those to your home. No matter what anyone else thinks.

Surround Yourself with Imperfect People

This may sound non-decorate-y, but don't underestimate this practice — it's actually a money-saving, time-saving, trouble-avoiding tip. Without honest, soul-caring, imperfect people in my life, it would be much harder, if not impossible, for me to be okay with imperfection in my home. Do you have those authentic friendships in your life? If your friends are people whom you constantly feel the need to impress and you spend a lot of time worrying about what they think of you, you'll never feel free to create a home that represents you and your family, and you may need to rethink your friends.

CHAPTER 13

Contentment

> *Do not spoil what you have*
> *by desiring what you have not;*
> *remember that what you now have was once*
> *among the things you only hoped for.*
>
> — EPICURUS

Everything You Need

It was the first luxurious home I had ever been in. I was newly married, Chad was a schoolteacher, we lived in The Apartment I Thought I Was Too Good For, and we had a new baby. One evening we attended a party at the home of a banker who was an alumni at the private school where my husband taught. That's where real, custom-made window treatments caught my eye and I never looked at windows the same way again.

As the normal guests were mingling, the window treatments and I got to know each other. They were interlined and felted and weighted and silk. They were longer and fuller than any curtain I had ever seen. I told the woman who owned the house that I loved her drapes because they made each window look as if it was wearing a pair of prom dresses. I'm sure that was the compliment she had in mind when she decided on them; it was the closest thing I had in my head to compare them to. I spent half the night molesting her window treatments and rubbing them against my face, and the other half wondering how much they cost and what I would need to sell to purchase me some.

After that night, I dreamed about beautiful window treatments. I started to pay attention to how much they cost and was amazed to find out that people can spend *thousands* of dollars on custom window treatments. Sometimes *thousands* of dollars *per window.* What world did I live in? I couldn't fathom spending that much on my windows. I started to feel I had nothing in common with the alumni and moms who sent their children to the school where my husband taught. I started feeling jealous of people whom I grouped into a sect called "people with money."

Once, a dear mom with children about five years older than mine spoke at a women's retreat at our church. She told a story about how they had just moved into a new home (my husband had pointed it out to me; in my mind it was a mansion, to say the least) and how she naturally was getting ready to have her custom window treatments ordered. Because that's what you do when you live in Macon, Georgia. You apparently cannot be caught dead without the proper window treatments.

She had a price quoted but didn't commit because she felt like the Lord was telling her to give away the money she had set aside for her window treatments. I could hardly keep up. Here's a woman who as far as I was concerned was a billionaire and I was supposed to feel her pain and be impressed that she was donating her precious window-treatment money?

> Each circumstance is different. It's not about a threshold but about the heart.

But, as the story went, the Lord came through and she miraculously won free window treatments for her home, so it all worked out in the end. Applause! Phew, I was so worried that she'd have to buy off-the-rack curtains. The suspense!

At that point in my life, I couldn't even buy McDonald's french fries. Here I was attending the oldest, steeped-in-tradition fancy Presbyterian church in town, my husband was working hard to teach the children of these families, yet we didn't have the money for me to grab lunch out, much less dream of treating my naked windows.

I left that retreat feeling cheated. And only focusing on one thing: me. I wanted more and better stuff. I liked pretty things and big houses and lined window treatments too. I'd give my window-treatment budget away too if it meant I still got to live in my pretty mansion. Life was so unfair.

Fast-forward about fifteen years to an almost non-memorable conversation with friends. We started talking about shoes, and a friend mentioned how she couldn't believe someone would pay $400 for a pair of shoes. The idea sickened her. She is a person who lives frugally, sacrificially, and purposely. Spending so much on a pair of shoes was clearly a waste. Someone else wondered out loud if it could be flat-out sinful for anyone to spend that much on shoes. I nodded in eager agreement — until I thought a little more.

I was suddenly aware of how strongly I disagreed that there is a threshold for sinning when it comes to the price of a pair of shoes. How much is too much? Is $80 okay to spend on shoes but not $280? What about $20? Is that wrong? What about

$2,000? Is $2,000 too much to spend on shoes? Each circumstance is different. It's not about a threshold but about the heart.

Oh and ouch. I remembered my own thoughts about the window-treatment speaker from years ago. I was so judgmental of her and her "sacrifice." Looking back, I see now that she was being generous with what God had called her to do. Who was I to judge? Would I have been as generous if I were in her place?

Today, this very afternoon, a mere eight hours after I wrote that story, I opened a letter from Jose, one of the boys we sponsor through Compassion International. He lives in Guatemala and wants us to get to know him. Here are his words: "I want to tell you that my house is very beautiful. The walls of my house are made of concrete blocks, the roof is made of tin sheets, and the floor is made of cement. We have water that we get from pipes ... I also want to tell you that we have electricity and it is good to have it because it helps me do my homework at night."

Then he asks, "How is your house like? Is your house big? Is your house beautiful? Are there trees close to where you live? How many windows does your house have? How many doors does your house have?"

Dear sponsor Chad and Myquillyn Smith:

I'm happy to write to you again. I want to tell you that my house is very beautiful. The walls of my house are made of concrete blocks, the roof is made of tin sheets, and the floor is made of cement. We have water that we get from pipes. On Saturdays I help to clean the house. I also want to tell you that we have electricity, and it is good to have it because it helps me to do my homework at night. I ask you to please pray for my family, pray that God takes care of us and protects us, pray that God keeps us wherever we go. I would like to know: How is your house like? Is your house big? Is your house beautiful? Are there trees close to where you live? Do you live close to the sea? How many windows does your house have? How many doors does your house have? Do you have pets? Do you play soccer? How many people live with you? What is your house made of? What is the roof of your house made of? I want to tell you that I live close to a cemetery. I send you greetings with love and I wish you blessings from God,

Jose

TOP LEFT A drawing Jose made of his own house   BOTTOM Translation of Jose's letter
TOP RIGHT Jose's letter

I've never wanted to lie to a child more in my life. Because part of me is thinking it will take me too long to count all of our precious windows. And do I count the ones in the guest room and front room? I mean, we hardly ever even use those rooms.

The irony of my thoughts doesn't escape me. I count the windows knowing I'll never answer his question because it is too extravagant. Thirty-two windows. We have thirty-two windows in our house.

I am the window-treatment lady living in what most people in the world would call a mansion. Yes, it's a rental, but it's two stories, it's more than two thousand square feet, and it has thirty-two windows. Would I be obedient if God asked me to give my window-treatment budget away?

The real question isn't whether it's right or wrong for me to live in a "big" house. The real question is, What am I doing with what I've been given?

A Slave to Circumstances

I used to be consumed by getting the right things to make our house beautiful. I was a slave to our circumstances, assuming that the right percentage of money, cute stuff, and God-given fabulous style would inevitably produce a magical, beautiful home I could be proud of. Until then, I couldn't fully love where I was.

But as I think back on all the different houses/condos/apartments/garages we've lived in, one thing is obvious. Every home has a silver lining.

The House with the Pink Carpet had a grapefruit tree in the back yard. *Grapefruit*, I tell you!

The Glorified Two-Car Garage was quaint and cozy with sloped ceilings.

The Two-Hundred-Year-Old Southern Mansion had five beautiful fireplaces and twelve-foot ceilings.

The Apartment I Thought I Was Too Good For had a sparkling-clean huge pool perfect for our two-year-old little boy and lush grass we never had to mow and pristine white walls begging for me to get creative.

The Big Rental House That Was So Not My Style had a twin-mattress-sized secret room under the stairs, complete with an outlet!

Our current rental home has wood and tile floors and a neighborhood pool. It's too good!

But at the time, I couldn't see these things. I was too busy criticizing what those homes were lacking to appreciate what they had.

This was especially true when we had to sell Our Imperfect Average Dream House and move into The Free Two-Bedroom Condo. Moving into a two-bedroom condo full of retirement-aged people was impossibly sad for me. I felt hopeless when I thought about my husband's job situation. Our boys, eight, six, and five years old at the time, shared one bedroom. We set up a twin bed with a trundle, and they rotated from those two beds to sleeping on the sofa that was also in their room. I felt like a loser mom because I had a child sleeping indefinitely on a sofa. I reminded them to try not to mention that at school.

When we first moved to the condo, some friends kept our family dog, Siler. At first we thought we'd be in the condo for only a few weeks. But weeks turned into months and finally we had to find Siler a new home. While my husband drove off with our boys' beloved pet, I took them out to the grassy hill outside the back door to play. They threw their Nerf football, and it hit the door of the elderly next-door neighbor. She came to the door ready for a fight. You would have thought they threw a brick through her window, mooned her with their hairy tattooed bottoms, and then flicked their cigarette ash into her flowerpot. How dare we felons with *children* live in these condos? She demanded to know why we were there and made sure I felt like we were second class.

I went inside and plopped on the bed and wept some of the deepest, hottest tears I've ever wept. My boys were giving away their pet, one child had to sleep on the sofa every night, our neighbors thought we were hellions because of our Nerf football fiascoes, not to mention the times we left the trash can out at the curb until nightfall. We went from living in our own beautiful home to living in a small condo where we felt like failures, and to top it off, my husband's job was still in question.

The Day a Stranger Died

Then came a life-altering day when I realized I was going about creating a beautiful, meaningful, purposeful home all wrong.

It was February 8, 2007. I was at an all-time low. I had never felt more sorry for myself. The Nerf football encounter was still fresh. Thinking about it immediately brought me to tears. We had a storage unit full of furniture and bikes and yard tools. We had to keep our boys in a private school that we couldn't afford because we had a signed contract. I drove a car we couldn't afford to sell because we were upside-down in the payments. I felt like such a fraud. To add to the depression, the boys kept asking me when we'd get the dog back. Then we sold our second car and Chad's parents let us borrow their pickup truck. He barely had a job, and it was becoming obvious that his current working situation was not what we hoped it would be.

Everyone gets to decide how happy they want to be, because everyone gets to decide how grateful they are willing to be.

— ANN VOSKAMP

Model and actress Anna Nicole Smith had been all over the news a few months earlier because she had a new baby girl. Days after her daughter was born, her twenty-year-old son was visiting her in the maternity ward and he suddenly died. Stories about Anna Nicole's life and her close relationship with her son surfaced. It was an all-around tragedy complete with drug accusations and people who live very differently from my friends and me. Nevertheless, a mother lost her son and no one could argue it was a sad turn of events. As a mom of all boys, I find that any tragic story involving sons of any age leaves an impression.

Meanwhile, I was in the midst of wallowing in how utterly horrible our lives had turned out. All our friends had great jobs and dogs in their back yards and, well, back yards. I was super busy working through scenarios of how I could control the outcome of our situation. Then on the news they announced that Anna Nicole Smith had been found dead in her hotel room. What? Wait, she's the mom of the new baby girl with the son who died in her hospital room just a few months ago.

I couldn't stop watching the coverage on Anna Nicole's life and death. Stories came out and a theme developed. It seemed she was a lonely woman, and friends and acquaintances implied she had always felt unloved. I cried harder that day than I can ever remember crying in my life. I wondered why I was crying over the death of this woman, a fellow mother I had barely heard of. But Anna Nicole Smith and you and I have something in common — we all want to love and we want to be loved.

In the midst of her tragedy, I realized what I had.

I had a great life. My little boys were healthy. My husband was doing everything he knew how to do to support us, and we knew that God was our ultimate provider. I realized that no matter what happened or where we went, it would be okay because we would all be together. Wherever we were, that was home. We were home. Home was us.

All my life I thought my dream was a pretty house, but really, my dream was to create a home. I realized that my quest for a dream house complete with hydrangeas and crown molding was sweet and well intentioned, but it wasn't the ultimate goal for my home. I needed to create something that didn't depend on money. Something I think you long for. Something I bet Anna Nicole Smith longed for too.

> Home. A place of rest while we are on this earth. A safe place for our children. A place to love and be loved. A place that is beautiful. A haven.

Home. A place of rest while we are on this earth. A safe place for our children. A place to love and be loved. A place that is beautiful. A haven.

With enough money, anyone can create a pretty house. But it takes intention to create a home.

I had been so foolish and wasteful. I finally came to terms with our shaky, we-have-no-idea-what-will-happen-next-week livelihood. I decided to trust that the God who is in charge of my eternal life could also be trusted with my everyday life.

Only then could I see the condo for what it was: a respite. Our lives were tumultuous, but the small condo began to feel like a safe little cocoon where I could fix a coupon-clipped yummy meal. It was a place where we would watch *Wheel of Fortune* together. It was a place where we would create some of our sweetest memories.

I realized my boys thought it was fun to share a room, and they actually fought over who got to sleep on the sofa at night. At less than half the size of our previous home, the condo was easy to keep clean. It still wasn't ours, the oven was old, the walls were orange, and there was no yard, but instead of seeing what it wasn't, I saw what it was. For the first time in my adult life, I found joy and peace in the midst of uncertainty and much less than perfect circumstances.

During our time in the condo, our situation actually got worse before it got better. But focusing on our blessings helped me give up trying to control the outcome. I learned to rest in the undone and the imperfect. My focus wasn't to find a job for my husband or pay off our debt. Instead, I made it my job to make home a peaceful

Are you waiting on your next house? The house that will be better and newer and bigger, the house that you will make into a beautiful home? This house you live in now, it's only temporary, it's not worth making it yours, so it sits untouched and unworthy. Months pass. Maybe even years. You put off having people over because this house doesn't truly represent your family. You waste time dreaming about the possibilities of the next house. Oh, the burden the next house carries, where all the living and enjoying and creating will happen. If only. Just remember: compared with your last house, this *is* your next house.

place for my husband to come home to and to find rest in the midst of the imperfect and crazy. That made all the difference.

God used the life and death of Anna Nicole Smith — Playmate of the Year, high school dropout, grieving mother — to shake me into reality, and I am so grateful. He can use whomever he wants to teach us things. And now Anna Nicole's daughter, little Dannielynn, has a dorky mom of three boys in North Carolina who prays for her.

Another World

The second life- and house-altering moment I had came five years, three months, and four days later from someone who couldn't be more opposite of Anna Nicole Smith. That was the day I met an awkward fifteen-year-old boy and visited his home in Tanzania. (I'm pretty sure he thought I was awkward too. Let's just say there was awkwardness all around.)

I had the opportunity to travel with Compassion International to Tanzania in the spring of 2012. We were a team of bloggers, and our job while we were there was to share with our online communities about the work of Compassion in that area.

Our family started sponsoring a fifteen-year-old boy right before the trip, so all I had was a photo of him and his name: Topiwo. I wasn't sure how to pronounce it, so I called him Topo to myself. We hadn't corresponded through letters yet, so we didn't really know each other.

After more than an hour's drive to the edge of Tanzania, I stepped off the bus and made my way around to a group of boys and one sassy girl. They were circled around a boy standing with his head down. He was smiling. I asked him his name, and it started with Top, which was the only part of his name I knew how to pronounce. There he was. Wearing the same clothes as in the picture. Tall and lanky. Staring down at the ground not knowing how to react. Still smiling.

When the children performed a song and dance for us, Topiwo was in the back row, completely off beat and uncoordinated. I couldn't help but adore him. I know,

TOP LEFT Topiwo with his friends, who are also in the Compassion program

BOTTOM LEFT Topiwo with his family outside their home

TOP RIGHT Me hugging Topiwo entirely too tightly

BOTTOM RIGHT Topiwo proudly standing next to the words he painted on the outside of his home

fifteen-year-old boys everywhere are cringing, but yes, this kid was *totally* adorable.

After the presentation, I pulled out a little photo book that my family had made for him and showed him pictures of my husband, boys, and dog.

Later our group of bloggers and guides and Topiwo went into the Compassion office and *he grabbed my hand.* I promise I did not in any way try to hint for him to hold my hand; I wanted to make sure I gave him space to be his own personality. But oh my word, he held my hand and sat by me in the office and he looked at those photos about twenty-three times while running his finger over parts of them and asking me what that thing was (a streetlight, a hockey goal, our three boys holding the one photo we had of Topiwo), and then he raised up the book and kissed it — right on the photo of our dog!

Next, a few of the bloggers, Compasson workers, and Topiwo and I were to walk to Topiwo's home to meet his family. I was excited, because you never really know a person until you've been in his home.

We had just spent four days walking over urban dirt roads and paths littered with trash, visiting children in concrete homes crammed close together as we turned away to hide our tears. Now, with Topiwo, we found ourselves in a pristine open plain at the foot of the mountains.

As we approached Topiwo's home, we saw that all the neighbors and family had gathered — children and men and women who all seemed to know that Topiwo's sponsor was there. They were gracious, mild mannered, smiling, all wanting to shake my hand.

Topiwo and his family lived inside a circular hut made of animal dung. It had a fire pit in the middle of its dirt floor and no windows at all except for one hole in the roof. It was extremely dark. It had two rooms, with thick branches like pillars holding up the structure from the inside and twigs and grass on the roof. I put my hand on one of the pillar branches. It was cool and sturdier than I expected.

ARTWORK created by Colette at Raw Art Letterpress

I knelt on the floor to give the family the few ridiculous gifts I'd brought. When I stood up, the knees of my jeans were damp with mud. The floor where they slept was wet.

As we got ready to leave, someone asked about the letters on the outside of Topiwo's hut. I hadn't noticed them before that. Turns out Topiwo painted them. I could make out his name and a number. I assumed he used the outside of his house to write some kind of harmless, fun teenage graffiti. Then someone asked what it said. Apparently, I had assumed wrong.

Topiwo had painted the words "Psalm 23" and then his name and the names of his family who lived with him in his mud hut. Do you remember how the Twenty-third Psalm starts? "The Lord is my shepherd; I have everything I need."

I had braced myself for shock and sadness and guilt and hopelessness over Topiwo's house. I knew his family had struggled to survive through drought until Compassion stepped in to help. But after visiting that beautiful dirt home, I didn't feel sad about where Topiwo lives. Unlike most of the homes we had visited, Topiwo's home was rich with love and community and joy and gracefulness. Richer than a lot of homes I see in our country. Rich with the contentment I want to have.

It was, in a word, breathtaking. I had been welcomed into a true home.

Topiwo knew. He knew what I so easily forget.

You don't have to wait for perfect conditions. Create your home now, wherever you are. You have everything you need.*

* If you would like to find out more about sponsoring a child with Compassion, see appendix 4.

CONCLUSION

Enjoying the Journey

Home interprets heaven.
Home is heaven for beginners.

— CHARLES HENRY PARKHURST

We don't want a pretty home just for the sake of a pretty home. Home is a place to come back to for rest. It's also a place to go out from to do everything else we're meant to do.

I long to create a home where all who enter can fully be themselves, and where all who leave can be more ready to live out their calling. After all, creating a beautiful home is a journey, not a destination. It is a privilege to live with beauty and creativity that inspire us so that we can inspire others to create in their unique ways.

So go, make your home a place of rest and joy and nurturing. It is from home that we become all we were created to be.

MYQUILLYN AND CHAD
and their boys, Landis, Cademon, and Gavin, with their dog, Jack

Acknowledgments

I'm eternally grateful for the people who put up with me through the years as this book was being lived out and written down.

Mom, who let me create elaborate Barbie houses and didn't make me clean them up every night. Dad, ever the optimist, who believed there was a book here ages ago. And my in-laws, who have been nothing but supportive.

Emily, the baby sister who is smarter, funnier, prettier, and a much better writer than me.

Caroline, Angela, Karrie, Reeve, Greta, Katie, and Maria, the most beautifully imperfect group of friends anyone could ask for.

Ellen, Tracey, Maggie, and Hayley, priceless heart friends.

The (in)courage writers, especially Lysa, the first person to see a book within the imperfection, and Ann, whom Zondervan listened to. I love this sisterhood.

Ashley and Andy, Chad and Sarah, and Caleb and Elaine, who agreed it was perfectly acceptable when I needed to sit upstairs and stare at a wall instead of joining our community group after a day in front of the computer.

The Nesting Place community. I was stunned and surprised at the gift of your friendship. You are kindred spirits whom I never even knew existed until I found that thing called a blog. I love you all so very much. Thank you for trusting some anonymous person on the internet who very well could have turned out to be a killer.

The Decorating Divas, a group of DIY bloggers who are ever supportive and generous. You listen to me whine and always give great advice.

Mrs. Barnhorst, my elementary art teacher. Now I know why you never told us what we were making until the end of the directions. You wanted us to enjoy the process.

Robin from Maxie B's. Thank you for taking a chance on me so many years ago.

Bonita, you got in my head and organized these thoughts. Elaine, Caroline, and Angela for reading the rough drafts and living through it.

Esther, I never would have pursued this if it hadn't been for your pursuing me. Thank you.

Carolyn, an angel-friend disguised as an editor.

The good people at Zondervan for taking a risk and seeing the beauty in the imperfect.

Lindsay, your artistry inspires me. Thank you for your beautiful cover art.

Landis, Cademon, and Gavin. Do you have any idea how much I love being a mom of boys? Thank you for not complaining every time I move the furniture.

Chad, the most encouraging man in the world, who has never shied away from risk. You cleaned toilets, washed dishes, and listened to me through this entire process without rolling your eyes. You are too good to me.

The Flexible, No-Rules Room Recipe

I often get asked how I go about creating the rooms in our home. I hesitate to write out a step-by-step process, because I hate rules, but I have figured out there are a few steps I've carried out in most of our rooms. Use the ideas that work for you and ignore the rest.

- Give up on perfection.
- Start with a real purpose. Decide how you want people to feel in the space.
- Embrace risk and remember that doing nothing is also a risk, maybe the biggest risk.
- Realize that every house has a silver lining and embrace what you have.
- Recognize the function, pieces, and meaningful beauty already in your home.
- Get advice from someone whose home you love to be in.
- Focus on one room at a time and quiet the space.
- Prepare your canvas (remove unnecessary items, paint the walls).
- Save for a bigger rug and use the rug to set the personality of a room.
- Makeover, DIY, hack, thrift, yardsale, move things around, barter, and be a smart buyer to fill in gaps.
- Don't be afraid to spend money, but don't assume you have to pay top dollar for everything. Don't charge it; it's not worth it.
- Overcompensate on lighting. Most rooms can use more than one lamp.
- MisTreat your windows or purchase drapes off the rack, unless having custom drapes is really your thing.
- Fill your walls with meaningful beauty, such as a gallery wall full of memories.
- Buy a plant. If it dies, that's okay. Buy another kind of plant until you find one that lives.
- Consider a signature piece.

- Sprinkle in a few opposites.
- Add a dash of quirk if your space is feeling too serious and if that makes you happy.
- Live in and enjoy your space. Don't fret when something breaks or gets scratched, because that is a sign of a life well lived. Yippie, you are doing it right!
- Welcome your friends into your home without apology.
- Surround yourself with imperfect people and things.
- Don't think of it as a room you hate. It's simply an unfinished room that you love.

The Imperfectionist Manifesto

WE BELIEVE that home should be the safest place on earth.

WE BELIEVE that home has a greater purpose than looking pretty.

WE BELIEVE that authenticity trumps perfection.

WE BELIEVE in mismatched sheets and unmade beds.

WE BELIEVE that the things in our house are there to serve us,
not the other way around.

WE BELIEVE that both pretty pillows and dogs should be on sofas.

WE BELIEVE that toys and homework and smelly shoes and
spilled milk are signs of life.

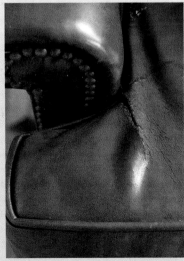

WE BELIEVE in using the good stuff now, not waiting for some future better purpose.

WE BELIEVE in handmade.

WE BELIEVE that contentment results not from stuff but from gratitude.

WE BELIEVE that decorating done good enough is better than decorating postponed.

WE BELIEVE that we are all creative because we are all made in the image of a creative God.

WE BELIEVE that it doesn't have to be perfect to be beautiful.

An Invitation

You are invited to join me and the beautiful community of imperfectionists daily at Nesting Place (thenester.com), where no one laughs at your mistakes and we embrace risk and talk about decorating without taking ourselves too seriously. There you'll find several years' worth of simple ideas for your home — easy changes that anyone (even people who hate to sew) can make. And now that you know perfection isn't the goal, you can better enjoy all of those DIY projects. Welcome home.

Here are a few other inspiring and creative home blogs you may want to check out:

http://allthingsthrifty.com

http://www.ana-white.com

http://www.beneathmyheart.net

http://buttonbirddesigns.com

http://www.centsationalgirl.com

http://creativehomebody.com

http://decorchick.com

http://diyshowoff.com

http://emilyaclark.blogspot.com

http://www.funkyjunkinteriors.net

http://www.thehandmadehome.net

http://www.homestoriesatoz.com

http://www.thehouseofsmiths.com

http://www.huntedinterior.com

http://www.infarrantlycreative.net

http://theinspiredroom.net

http://www.justagirlblog.com

http://knockoffdecor.com

http://theletteredcottage.net

http://www.lifeingraceblog.com

http://www.makelyhome.com

http://missmustardseed.com

http://myblessedlife.net

http://www.thenester.com

http://www.notjustahousewife.net

http://www.perfectlyimperfectblog.com

http://www.prettyhandygirl.com

http://www.remodelaholic.com

http://roadkillrescue.net

http://www.sawdustgirl.com

http://www.theshabbycreekcottage.com

http://shabbynest.blogspot.com

http://www.songbirdblog.com

http://southernhospitalityblog.com

http://tatertotsandjello.com

http://www.thriftydecorchick.blogspot.com

http://www.vintagerevivals.com

http://www.younghouselove.com

Compassion International

For about the cost of one family meal out per month (or, if you are me, the cost of a lamp), you can help change the life of a child. Compassion International's mission is to release children from poverty in Jesus' name. It's made possible by people like you and me who are simply willing to sponsor a child. I've seen firsthand the life-changing benefits for entire families that come from child sponsorship. It's the best money I've ever spent.

To read more about my trip to Tanzania with Compassion, as well as more about Compassion's financial integrity and the lives they are touching, visit *compassion.com* or scan this QR code:

Stop by and say hi on Instagram.
@thenester

Create the home you've always wanted.
Use it the way you've always dreamed.

Learn more about Myquillyn's courses, community,
and events at AcademyofHome.com

Academy
HOME of

THE NEST FEST

A yearly festival with a thousand of my favorite people in the world: makers, pickers, curators, farmers, foodies, musicians, and artists of all sorts.

Learn More at TheNester.com

Cozy Minimalist Home

More Style, Less Stuff

Myquillyn Smith, New York Times *Bestselling Author*

Cozy Minimalist Home goes beyond pretty and sets up your home for true connection and rest without using more resources, money, and stuff than needed.

After reading Myquillyn Smith's first book, *The Nesting Place,* women everywhere were convinced that it doesn't have to be perfect to be beautiful, and they found real contentment in their homes. But how does a content imperfectionist make actual design decisions?

Cozy Minimalist Home is the answer to that question. Written for the hands-on woman who'd rather move her own furniture than hire a designer, this is the guidance she needs to finish every room of her house one purposeful design decision at a time. With people, priorities, and purpose in mind, anyone can create a warm, inviting, cozy, and beautiful home that transcends the trends.

You'll have the tools to transform your home starting with what you already have, and using just enough of the right furniture and décor to create a home you're proud of in a way that honors your personal priorities, budget, and style. In *Cozy Minimalist Home,* Myquillyn Smith helps you:

- Realize your role as the curator of your home who makes smart, stylish design choices
- Finally know what to focus on and what not to worry about when it comes to your home
- Discover the real secret to finding your unique style—it has nothing to do with those style quizzes
- Understand how to find a sofa you won't hate tomorrow
- Deconstruct each room and then re-create it step by step with a fail-proof process
- Create a pretty home with more style and less stuff—resulting in backward decluttering!
- Finish your home and have it looking the way you've always hoped so you can use it the way you've always dreamed

Cozy minimalism isn't about going without or achieving a particular new, modern style. Nope. It's simply a mindset that helps you get whatever style YOU LOVE with the fewest possible items.

Available in stores and online!

Welcome Home

A Cozy Minimalist Guide to Decorating and Hosting All Year Round

Myquillyn Smith, New York Times *Bestselling Author*

Decorating for each season doesn't have to be over-whelming or expensive. Your home can be festive, stylish, and cozy with minimal effort and a limited budget—just ask The Nester! In *Welcome Home*, Myquillyn Smith guides you through creating and enjoying a seasonally decorated home with more style and less stuff.

No matter what the world says, embracing the seasons does not require bins of factory-made décor or loads of time. In fact, it's possible to decorate for each season without frustration, going overboard, or blowing your budget.

Drawing from the cozy-minimalist principles in *Cozy Minimalist Home*, stylist and *New York Times* bestselling author Myquillyn Smith will help you create a home that's fresh, meaningful, beautiful, and (bonus!) always ready to host. With engaging how-tos and inspiring photos, she guides you step by step through purposeful design decisions to cultivate a space where loved ones gather, meaningful connections are celebrated, and lasting memories are made.

Myquillyn's realistic and down-to-earth design tips will teach you how to:

- Seasonalize your living spaces with simple, actionable steps
- Cultivate easy, seasonal rhythms of change in your home
- Incorporate the beauty of the natural world through the five senses
- Feel confident in volunteering your house for gatherings, parties, and impromptu get-togethers
- Know what to focus on and what not to worry about as a relaxed and confident hostess

Bigger than the latest and greatest trends, *Welcome Home* aims to usher in the seasons without using more resources, money, or stuff than needed.

Available in stores and online!